Nehru and Modern India

An Anatomy of Nation-building

Nehru and Modern India

An Anatomy of Nation-building

Edited by

G. Gopa Kumar

Honorary Director, UGC-Nehru Studies Centre,
University of Kerala, Thiruvananthapuram

New Century Publications
New Delhi, India

NEW CENTURY PUBLICATIONS
4800/24, Bharat Ram Road,
Ansari Road, Daryaganj,
New Delhi – 110 002 (India)

Tel.: 011-2324 7798, 4358 7398, 6539 6605
Fax: 011-4101 7798
E-mail: indiatax@vsnl.com • info@newcenturypublications.com
www.newcenturypublications.com

Editorial office:
LG–7, Aakarshan Bhawan,
4754-57/23, Ansari Road, Daryaganj,
New Delhi – 110 002

Tel.: 011-4356 0919

First Published: **July 2010**

ISBN: **978-81-7708-242-5**

Published by New Century Publications and printed at Salasar
Imaging Systems, New Delhi.

Designs: Patch Creative Unit, New Delhi.

PRINTED IN INDIA

ABOUT THE BOOK

Pandit Jawaharlal Nehru—the First Prime Minister of Independent India—was the embodiment of spirit and ideals of democracy, socialism, secularism, nationalism, equality and social justice.

Estimating the contemporary significance and historical relevance of Nehru will always remain a challenging task for the students of social sciences. Nehru continues to remain a crucial link between the evolution of India's contemporary nationalism and the transition towards a middle-range power among the countries of the modern world. Along with other great stalwarts of freedom movement, Nehru was successful and practical in envisioning a modern India. Given the complex social, cultural, political and historical background of the Continent, this was a tremendous task. In the post-Independence scenario, Nehru was able to provide a strong foundation to the political system and clear directions to foreign and domestic policies. Despite the fast changing nature of the international system, Nehruvian perspectives are very relevant even today.

This book contains 12 papers, authored by eminent scholars, which critically examine the policies pursued by Nehru in shaping modern India.

EDITOR'S PROFILE

Dr. G. Gopa Kumar is presently Professor and Chairman of the Department of Political Science, Dean of Social Sciences and Honorary Director of UGC-Nehru Studies Centre, University of Kerala, Thiruvananthapuram. He has published 7 books and 125 research articles. He was a Senior Fellow of the Australia-India Council, Melbourne (2009), Shastri Fellow in Canada (Calgary, 2000 and McGill, 2006), Salzburg Fellow in Austria (1998), Fulbright Scholar in USA (1998), International Visiting Fellow in USA (1996), UGC-Cultural Exchange Programme in France (1990), UGC-Research Scientist (1988-89). He was a visiting faculty of Claremont Graduate University, California, USA (1998 and 2003) and University of Calgary, Alberta, Canada (2001).

CONTENTS

PREFACE

Estimating the contemporary significance and historical relevance of a great nation-builder like Pandit Jawaharlal Nehru will remain a challenging task to the students of social sciences. Nehru continues to remain a crucial link between the evolution of India's contemporary nationalism and the transition towards a middle range power among the countries of the modern world. Along with other great stalwarts of freedom movement, Nehru was successful and practical in envisioning a modern India. Given the complex social, cultural, political and historical background of the Continent, this was a tremendous task. In the post-Independence scenario, Nehru was able to provide a strong foundation to the political system and clear directions to foreign and domestic policies. Despite the fast changing nature of the international system, Nehruvian perspectives are very relevant even today. As a democrat, he encouraged criticism and even wrote anonymous article warning the people "to prevent Nehru from becoming a dictator". Nehru would have no problem in appreciating his critics even if he would have been around, today. Of course, there were shortcomings on some of his policies and decisions and when we cross-examine these issues in the present day context, the criticisms become much sharper.

This work is the first publication by the UGC-funded Nehru Studies Centre functioning in the University of Kerala, Thiruvananthapuram. The Centre came into existence in March 2005 and during the last 4 years, the Centre has been able to organize a number of academic events. I express my gratitude to all the paper writers for contributing their ideas which finally helped in strengthening this volume. Gratitude is also due to all the colleagues in the Department: Dr. J. Prabhash, Mr. C. Muraleedharan, Dr. Shaji Varkey, Dr. A. Basheer and Dr. K.M. Sajad Ibrahim for sustaining academic ambience. I acknowledge the services of Anju Joseph, Research Assistant in the Department who helped in proofreading and correcting the drafts at various stages. Finally, I am grateful to the members of my family, especially my wife Mrs. Jayasree Gopa Kumar, for providing all moral support and encouragement in the completion of this work at a stressful time in life.

June 2010   **Dr. G. Gopa Kumar**
Thiruvananthapuram

CONTRIBUTORS

A.K. Pasha — Professor, Centre for West Asian and African Studies, School of International Studies, Jawaharlal Nehru University (JNU), New Delhi.

Aparajita Gangopadhyay — Assistant Professor, Centre for Latin American and International Studies, Goa University, Goa.

P. Arjun Rao — Specialist in Public Administration and formerly Consulting Editor of ICFAI Journal of Public Administration.

G. Gopa Kumar — Professor and Head, Department of Political Science, University of Kerala, Thiruvananthapuram.

K.R. Singh — Formerly Professor, Centre for West Asian and African Studies, School of International Studies, Jawaharlal Nehru University (JNU), New Delhi.

L.C. Jain — Social activist, freedom fighter and a former member of the Planning Commission, Government of India.

M.J. Vinod — Professor, Department of Political Science, University of Bangalore, Bangalore.

Rahul Tripathi — Reader and Head, Department of Political Science, Goa University, Goa.

B. Ramesh Babu — Formerly Professor and Head, Department of Political Science, University of Bombay.

R.L.M. Patil — Formerly Professor and Head, Department of Political Science, University of Bangalore, Bangalore.

Sudhir Jacob George — Formerly Professor, Department of Political Science, University of Hyderabad, Hyderabad.

V. Bijukumar — Assistant Professor, Department of Political Science, North-Eastern Hill University, Shillong, Meghalaya.

INTRODUCTION BY THE EDITOR

This book is the effort of the Nehru Studies Centre established in 2005 with the support of University Grants Commission in the Department of Political Science, University of Kerala. It is the first publication by the Centre and we plan to bring out more volumes in future. The goals of the Centre include training students and youth in developing the spirit and ideals of democracy, socialism, secularism, nationalism, equality and social justice—all these were close to Pandit Jawaharlal Nehru. The Centre proposes to promote Nehruvian values and ideals among the future generation of the country. This, in turn, is expected to shape and strengthen nation-building process. During the last 4 years, the Centre has conducted three major conferences besides organizing lectures by visiting faculty on themes that are of vital importance to the thinking and practice of Jawaharlal Nehru.

In one of my intellectual encounters abroad, I recall how a colleague from Nigeria commented on the vital democratic space created in India by the great leaders of India's freedom struggle. He said, "Unlike Nigeria, India produced a strong battery of leaders during the freedom movement, trained in Gandhian and Nehruvian values and this impacted positively upon the future generations of your country". He added with a smile, "Like in a good cricket match, if the first four or five batsmen bat very well, the huge score accomplished by the team will be impregnable and therefore cannot be easily defeated by the rival team. Your leadership invested so much on nation-building efforts and the foundation of the country therefore became strong. Whereas in Nigeria, our leadership had ditched us quite often and the legacy of freedom movement, however small it was, got fabricated". He was certainly right, and no wonder Nigeria had undergone series of *coup-d' etat* which destroyed the potentialities of shaping a civil society in a young country.

Therefore, it is all the more true that among the post-colonial societies, India holds a pride of place. The relevance and contribution of the leaders of freedom movement— Mahatma Gandhi, Pandit Jawaharlal Nehru, Sardar Vallabhai Patel, C. Rajagopalachari, Acharya Kripalani, Maulana Azad, Rajendra Prasad, G.B. Pant, Netaji Subhash Chandra Bose, Lal Bahadur Shastri, B.R. Ambedkar and a large set of others – are to be studied which would not only rekindle the spirit of national unity but also enable the public to estimate the values and challenges of nation-building process. Indeed, for many western scholars the emergence of a modern India with a complex social and colonial history is really baffling. Certainly, it was not an easy task to unite and integrate the 565 princely states and other areas and regions that were under direct British rule. The ethnic, linguistic, regional, religious and caste divisions in a huge country are major challenges, especially, in a young political system of parliamentary democracy. Not only that India emerged over the years as a plural society but also it could introduce liberal vales such as parliamentary democracy, secularism and federalism. Despite the many complex issues awaiting urgent solutions, India could successfully celebrate her electoral democracy. The verdict of the 15th Lok Sabha election further vindicates this argument.

In this context it would be interesting if we could research on the multifaceted dimensions of Nehruvian contributions to the development of modern India. Although critics would attack him on many issues like the setback in China policy, issue of Tibet imbroglio, problems in Kashmir, the limitations of non-alignment, issues and developments that led to the Partition, failure of public sector in contributing to socio-economic development, we could on the other side point out that the flip sides of many these problems were beyond his control. Declaring himself as the "first servant of the people of India", he set himself as a role- model among the politicians of a newly independent country. Again, his refusal to accept Gandhiji's advice to dissolve the Indian National Congress and transform it into a *Lok Sevak Sangh* on the eve of independence was found to be more valid. Indeed, a political vacuum would have developed, if the Indian National Congress was dissolved in 1947 and consequently India would have faced an anarchic divergent party system with disastrous results. It is understandable that the era of one-party dominance is over now and India is rapidly heading towards multi-party system within the framework of coalition politics. This also enabled opposition parties to come up within a reasonable time frame with the essential political experience needed for governance and accountability.

At the domestic front, Nehru's vision had a long standing impact. His perspectives on democratic socialism, state led planning process, establishment of Planning Commission, launching of the mechanism for rural development, initiative for modernizing agriculture and educational system etc. could be seen in the early fifties itself. He declared India's unique commitment to establish a 'socialistic pattern of society' in the Parliament on 21 December, 1954 and followed it up by the AICC resolution at Avadi in early 1955. The mixed economy model was suitable for a developing nation like India and the country was ready to accept the advantages of both capitalism and socialism. Nehru felt that the state should play the crucial role in development and attributed high credentials and role to both the bureaucracy and public sector. He used the traditional idioms to communicate with the masses on emphasizing the utility of modern tools and institutions. He realized the importance of setting up mega industries and usher in industrial growth so as to transform the traditional society into a modern one.

While "agriculture cannot wait", Nehru was particularly sensitive to the cause of industrial development. Indeed, Gandhiji and Nehru differed on the question of industrial development .He was against rapid industrialization and instead suggested the growth of cottage industries. Nehru, on the other hand, anticipated the scope for industrial development in shaping the future of the people and the nation. Although Dr. B.R. Ambedkar differed with Nehru on many issues, he appreciated Nehru's commitment to industrial development and expressed his differences with Gandhiji. As an institution-builder Nehru was also able to set up numerous scientific institutions all over the country.

As the first Minister for External Affairs, Nehru was responsible for developing an independent foreign policy for the country. Reviewing the problem of cold war and bi-polar politics, Nehru designed the equidistance concept towards big powers while engaging with them in all possible fronts. Along with Nasser, Sukarno, Tito, Nehru played a crucial role in shaping the policy of non-alignment and institutionalized the Non-Aligned Movement. Despite the setback with China, India received the support of USA on many occasions, although American Secretary of State Dallas attacked Non-Alignment as an *immoral force*. Similarly, USSR was India's natural ally on vital sectors. When viewed from contemporary international system, the past policies may look irrelevant but during the cold war era those were very practical and dynamic policies. Unlike Pakistan, India did not join any military camp and could pursue an independent foreign policy. India also contributed to the UN efforts in peace-keeping by sending its forces to many war-torn areas.

Of course, one can understand the critics' view on Nehru's under estimating of Chinese tactics towards India. Hence Nehru shared the blame along with V.K. Krishna Menon on the military setback with China in October 1962. But politically India could convince the UN and the international community that MacMohan line constitutes the legitimate international boundary between China and India. Although China rejected this position, and further made claims over some areas in Arunachal Pradesh, the Indian position received more international acceptance. It may also be recalled that Nehru was sincere in his plan for having a friendly neighbour. He realistically considered the geographical aspects and the trouble of having a hostile neighbour with a long frontier .The Panch Sheel, though was not completely successful, was a product of this vision. Given the development in the 21st century, both China and India have emerged as major players at the economic, political and security spheres. China today has a strong military power sophisticated in every sense and India is closely watching her strategic and economic interests and game plans in South Asia, South East Asia and Africa.

It is also not clear as to who would have advised Nehru in taking up the Kashmir problem to the UN Security Council. Again, Nehru ordered the stopping of Indian army's surge towards the Pakistan Occupied Kashmir. The much promised plebiscite on Kashmir has become a non- starter. The Kashmir imbroglio continues to affect both India and Pakistan. Significantly, it has complicated the domestic politics of the two countries.

Another major criticism with regard to the Partition from certain quarters was that if Nehru had yielded to some of the demands of the Muhammad Ali Jinnah, partition of the country would have been avoided. But it was too much an attempt to simplify the historical as well as the unexpected events that led to the division of the sub-continent and the violence that followed. Again, Nehru's firm commitment to secularism and his strong objection to Jinnah's demand for setting up communal electorates, following the Government of India Act 1935, is very much evident before us to analyze the situation.

Undoubtedly, Jawaharlal Nehru would remain a towering personality in Indian socio-political landscape. When one would review the achievements and setbacks, the balance is undoubtedly in favour of Nehru's accomplishments. It is true that Nehru failed on certain areas, aspects and policies. But he played a phenomenal role in providing a strong socio-economic foundation to India's growth and development. This is more visible in the present era of neo-liberal order. He was a statesman, institution-builder, secularist, pacifist, democrat with scientific and humanist values and temperament. As a true democrat he appreciated dissent and yielded to his critics' point of view. He was responsible for taking India to the pride of place among the nations of the world. Being a disciple of Gandhi, peace and moral values prevailed on him tremendously. His own vision and instinct, besides the international exposure he received, influenced his perspectives considerably. Modern India owes a great to this unique nation-builder of the 20th century.

Given the radically altered international system, many of the basic postulates of Nehruvian ideas are receiving heavy challenges. Two major principles, viz. non-alignment and socialistic pattern of society, with state led planning process, are now at the receiving end. It is a debatable point whether India could continue to stick on to the policies of non-alignment and planned development in the 21st century. The international system in the present century is totally different from that of what we saw in the post World War II era. Many of the principles like balance of power, bi-polarism, ideological competition between two super powers, equilibrium in the UN Security Council etc. had radically changed. The present day world witnesses the rise and decline of unipolarism, emergence of multilateralism in global politics, increased role of China, India, European Union, Russia etc, the rise of international terrorism, religious fundamentalism and challenges to national security, environmental degradation and climate change etc. The march of free market capitalism since 1991 and the decline of Communism had fundamentally altered the global system. No country can stay aloof from these developments. It is exactly in this context we can notice the challenges to the traditional principles of non-alignment and centrally planned economic development. Theoretically, both are questionable today.

Nevertheless, one could not ignore the role and major contributions of the Nehruvian state. At least, three generations of Indian population were benefited from it. It had contributed significantly in improving the levels of health, education, food, housing, employment etc. At the same time, it would be incorrect to argue that every section had been benefited from these policies. To be sure, more than one-third of the population was deprived from these developments. Once again, the debate of social justice and inclusive development comes to the forefront. When Gandhiji appealed for 'sarvodaya' and Nehru for 'social justice', they definitely had the idea of inclusive development upper most in their minds. Hence Gandhian and Nehruvian values are still relevant but in a different dimension. We need to explore the potentialities of Nehruvian studies in this context.

Nehru's development strategy was based on three pillars- planning for industrial and agricultural growth, a public sector to develop strategic industries and mixed economy, argues A.K. Pasha in his paper **Nehru, Mixed Economy and Aspects of Foreign Policy**. Although Nehru sought aid and assistance from the West he could not get it substantially because of his foreign policy stances. Nehru tried to promote equality and socialism and build an independent self-reliant economy. The author strongly argues that Nehru's external and internal policies are closely interlinked and therefore he emphasised secularism, communal peace, harmony along with socialism and non-alignment. He reviews his foreign policy perspectives and compares Nehru's role in leading India with Abdul Nasser of Egypt. Not only Nehru took a strong position against Israel over Palestine question, he also developed close ties with Egypt which in turn neutralized Palestine offensive against India in the WANA region, over the Kashmir issue. However, with the end of Cold War, Indian foreign policy underwent a reorientation. Despite the emergence of unipolar world, the author believes that the world is moving towards multipolar world. The plan initiated by Nehru had placed India today as a leading power in the world. It developed an economic pattern of its own and has now entered a period of high economic growth. But what Indian leaders since Nehru's death have ignored is the soft power-generating dynamo of peace making that Nehru did so ably even India's 'hard power' was limited. Nehru contributed considerably for strengthening modern India and the present Indian leadership should add more inputs to it.

Aparajita Gangopadhyay in her paper **From Nehru to** *Pravasi Bharathiya Diwas*: **Changing Contours of India's Diaspora Policy** presents aspects of continuity and change in India's policy towards its diaspora. In the age of Globalization, diaspora plays a crucial role in linking up ties between the motherland and foster land. The potentialities for strengthening cultural, economic and political relationships are indeed great and diaspora could serve the role of a positive catalyst in such relationships. The major objective of this paper is to understand the implications of diaspora and government initiatives vis-à-vis noticeable shifts in the foreign policy matrix of the Indian state. Pandit Nehru did not offer the foundation for developing diaspora roles and considered overseas Indians as an external entity outside the purview of Indian domestic and foreign policy formulations. He advised his overseas brethren to integrate themselves within their host countries. This policy of impassiveness continued till the 1980's. The author reviews the antecedents of the Indian diaspora, one of the largest in the world, with its presence in all continents. She reviewed the limited role of diaspora during the Nehruvian era and the transformation that occurred with the liberalization policies. The 'New' diaspora policy was brought by BJP through the NDA regime. This shift could be identified with the pro-active foreign policy of the recent period which is pragmatic. The policy shift has a class character in the changed global scenario where the role of NRI's is appreciated by the ruling elite in India. But there are many controversial issues to be tacked and the real economic contribution of NRI's are very nominal.

P. Arjun Rao's paper **Nehruvian Legacy: Democratic Socialism and Strategy of Economic Development - An Appraisal** attempts to describe the economic conditions prevailing in India during 1950's. The economic scenario was depressing and miserable with mass poverty, illiteracy, feudal domination in agriculture, untrained labour, poor transport and communication system and unemployment. Prime Minister Nehru chose industrialisation as a strategy for development without ignoring agriculture and small scale industry. Heavy investments were made in public sector to achieve growth and production with equi-distribution and social justice. He chose democratic socialism, a synthesis of both the systems, i.e. democracy and socialism, for development and fuller life of the society. The author concludes by arguing that Nehru-Mahalanobis model of economic development could not only build strong infrastructure for development but provide effective foundation for future sustainable growth and development. Despite mistakes and limitations, the policies pursued by Nehru were very useful for the country and it helped in laying a strong economic and democratic foundation. Opposition parties who were critics of these policies followed the same line which they opposed and this itself justified the extent of rationalism involved in Nehruvian policies. The author also point out that most underdeveloped and developing countries still look to Nehru's economic plans to achieve self-sufficiency and to pursue independent policies.

The Indian National Congress had served numerous roles in nation building process—major vehicle of freedom struggle, instrument of social change, the consensus oriented political platform for Indian masses and elites and above all the role of the strongest national party of India. G. Gopa Kumar in his paper **Jawaharlal Nehru and the Congress Party of India** reviews the historical and contemporary role of Congress in Indian political system with particular focus on Pandit Nehru. He was the crucial link between Gandhiji and traditional Indian society. The paper discusses the nature of inner party democracy during the early phase and the subsequent period, socialist and secular ideas of Nehru and its impact in the Congress Party, the unique coalition character of Congress

Party, etc. The author compares the leadership and institutional roles in the Congress Party during the pre and post-independent period. Both Congress as an institution and Nehru as a personality complemented each other. Neither could dispense with the other and it provided a fine tuning in shaping political culture. The author cites with evidences that Nehru was not at all responsible for the development of dynasty politics in the Congress Party. With the great split in 1969, Nehruvian values started depleting from the Congress organisation. The fading Nehruvian legacy in the contemporary political process is really painful, concludes the author.

K.R. Singh's paper on **Nehru and India's Foreign Policy** surveys Nehru's vision of modern India and how the country was destined to locate its new role as an emerging major power in the modern world. He classifies Nehru's foreign policy in three phases—pre-Independence, Independence (1947-1964) and post Nehru period. K.R. Singh identified several foreign policy challenges during Nehru's era but focus attention on four issues – the Kashmir question, challenges of 1954, the liberation of Goa and the 1962 war with China. Particularly, the Kashmir question and the Chinese war became very controversial but the author holds that "those policies though militarily a failure was politically correct." Nehru was proved wrong on his perception towards China. Nehru felt that he was betrayed not only by the Chinese but also by the world.

The author thinks that India did not learn the lesson despite the experience of 1962. "Probably India needed a 'lesson' on the intricacies of 'sama', 'dana', 'danda', 'bheda'. Diplomacy of peace alone can never be the basis of foreign policy. He highlights Nehruvian contribution to the development of science and technology in his vision of India as an emerging power. Nehru, according to the author, was against foreign dependence in science and technology especially in nuclear field. Nehru's framework of India's foreign policy continued to influence decision makers even after his death. Despite the changing domestic and international environment, it is crucial to retain independence of decision making as a vital element in foreign policy making. He concludes by asking the question, "Are Indian policy makers, while paying lip services to Nehru, really adhering to these basic postulates of an "independent" foreign policy"?

L.C. Jain's paper on **Glimpses of Jawaharlal Nehru** is an attempt to recall his own journey of working with Nehru on various public issues and developments. The journey begins from his involvement in the students' movement during the freedom struggle. L.C. Jain reviews Nehru's influence in Asia and the world. The author covers a wide range of activities in which Nehru was involved like the shaping of the Indian Constitution, State Reorganisation Commission, planned economic development, National Development Council, etc. He points out that it was Nehru's imagination and drive that shaped the dynamic factor of India's economic stability, viz the planned economic development. On the whole, the paper survey Nehru's contribution in vital areas of development, freedom, peace, equality, etc. He also narrates Nehru's efforts in preventing chaos and offering rehabilitation measures to the people following the Partition. L.C. Jain recollects his experiences in the relief camps, co-operative farms organized for landless refugees and other community efforts in the post-partition period. The author realises that a lot of learning flowed in from real life in this challenging situation.

As a great democrat Nehru did not take crucial policy decisions single-handedly. This is especially true of foreign policy decisions as well. Many great personalities influenced Nehru's vision just as Nehruvian ideas influenced others. M.J. Vinod's paper on **The *Menonian* Influence on *Nehruvian* Foreign and Security Policy** highlights the prominent role played by V.K. Krishna Menon on Nehru since 1954. He was Nehru's right hand man in foreign policy matters and Nehru-Menon axis could be seen in areas and issues related to

Commonwealth, India's position on Korean War, the Goa episode, India-China relations, India's military preparedness etc. The author also highlights the flip side Nehru-Menon axis. As a matter of fact Nehru-Menon relationship became very controversial in the political discourse after India's setback with the Chinese in 1962. Many leaders close to Nehru found Krishna Menon as a great source of influence on Nehru which landed up Nehru in serious troubles. A section of the media also backed this group and raised allegation against Menon which finally led to his exit from the Cabinet. M.J. Vinod concludes that it would be an error to exaggerate the 'Menonian' influence on the, 'fundamental character' and 'direction' of 'Nehruvian' foreign policy. The author feels that despite Menon's power and influence, he did not change the course of foreign policy in any other direction. Nevertheless, Nehru-Menon axis had attracted international attention and controversies both abroad and inside.

Foreign policy of any country is not a static phenomenon and this is certainly true of a huge and complex country like India, getting ready to emerge as a major global player in the Twenty-first century. One can certainly witness a definite shift from 'idealism to pragmatism'. Rahul Tripathi's paper **Interpreting Nehru in the Context of India's New Foreign Policy** argues that Nehru provides the ideological framework from which continuities and changes in foreign policies can be dissected and inferences drawn on the ideological or pragmatic shifts. The paper discusses Nehru's vision and Nehruvianism and then come back to understand the shifts that had taken place in the recent period. As a counter point to Nehruvianism, the author highlights that India's recent economic and strategic resurgence has taken place after shunning the 'Nehruvian middle path' and moral ambiguity that was characteristic of India's foreign policy. According to some scholars 'the 1998 nuclear test provided the defining movement when India shed its Nehruvian baggage. Moreover, in the post-Nehruvian context, India's commitment to Non-alignment and Third

Worldism became more of a ritual. Interestingly, the author believes that Nehru would have certainly been pretty quick to accept the changes in the contemporary world. Although he would have faced the dilemma of choosing between a new ally and an old partner, nevertheless he would have been less ambiguous than India' present leadership. He would have supported the multilateral trends shaping a cross developing nations. He concludes by suggesting that it is up to the present day leadership to convert Nehru's ideas into greater political reality. A great volume of pragmatism was inherent in Nehru's ideas, he concluded.

B. Ramesh Babu's paper, **The Nehruvian Legacy: The Eternal** and **the Ephemeral in Foreign Policy** attempts to look at the Nehruvian legacy with focus on the traditions of Nehru's foreign policy. The author holds that Pandit Nehru and pre and post-independent India were so intertwined that they cannot be separated. No democratic leader in the history enjoyed popular support than Nehru as the architect of India's foreign policy. Nehru was influenced b India's cultural heritage and civilization. But he feels that India drifted away from idealism and we lost our representational legitimacy as the spokesman of the poor people in the world. Ramesh Babu criticizes that after 1962 non-alignment blossomed into bi-alignment—the non-alignment became more helplessly integrated into the paradigm of the super power politics. With the collapse of Soviet Union, non-alignment became irrelevant and conceptually meaningless. He explains the dilemmas and challenges of the present day world. India under the spells of globalization and liberalization is anxious to join the elite arms exporting club. He fears that India is getting lost in the enveloping sea of aping the west. The profit driven growth is simply not concerned with equity and this realisation is there with decision makers. Given this complex scenario, can we discard the ephemeral in the Nehru legacy and revitalise the eternal in it? Ramesh Babu strongly believes that there are many eternal strands in Nehruvian legacy worthy of preservation and revitalisation. The revival of the eternal in the Nehruvian legacy is the urgent need of the hour.

R.L.M. Patil in his paper **Jawaharlal Nehru's Dialectics** points out that as a speaker and writer Pandit Jawaharlal Nehru was a gifted person. He had his own way of convincing his readers and listeners of the correctness of his opinion. He did this through a method for arguing against himself. He invited his audience to share his inner dialogue. He did not appear to attack his detractors headlong. Instead he appears to agree with his opponent's view point in the beginning of his argument. In the end, however, he shows his opposition and takes a stand which was more of a reconciliatory nature than scoring a triumphant point. He appears to absorb contradictions rather than breakdown the conflict. His well stated positions on several important issues can be cited to prove the skill of his argument. Some of these are India's position on the Kashmir question, India-China border problem, Commonwealth, States-reorganisation, socialism, judiciary Vs. parliament, relevance of Gandhi, and his own role as Prime Minister vis-à-vis his cabinet ministers. One finds that in all these Nehru is not prima facie consistent in his view. According to the author a deeper examination would, however, reveal that he was in argument with himself, unable to take a fundamental and ultimate position. He was preparing his defence in advance in case of failure of his approach. In his autobiography he would admit to this mindset, concludes R.L.M. Patil.

Sudhir Jacob George in his paper **Nehru, Democracy and the North-East** analyses how Nehru had to grapple with several intractable problems in the frontier areas of North-East. Nehru being a democrat and a strong supporter of the marginalised communities never advocated a military solution to the Naga problem. Nehru felt that it was politically expedient to create among the tribes a feeling of kinship with the rest of the country. He laid emphasis on improving infrastructure rather than in enforcing law and order. Besides his humane approach, the greatest contribution of Nehru to the North-East and its distinct people has been his formulation of five fundamental principles in relation to the North-East Frontier Agency (NEFA). The author believes that building up a strong democratic India alone can bring security, peace and prosperity to every section of the Indian society. Positive steps are needed to address the grievances of the people of the disturbed states of the North East. He wonders, how long will the armed forces of our country train their guns against their own people? The Nehruvian approach is very important here. Only democratic practices and settlement on the basis of equity and justice can solve the outstanding problems in the North-East. The Sixth Schedule of the Indian Constitution which strengthened the democratic ethos in the political process was designed by Nehru, he added.

Nehruvian model has to be seen in a historical context and was a product of a long process of interaction and accommodation of diverse ideas and ideologies, argues V. Bijukumar in his paper **Contextualizing Nehruvian Development: Democratic Compulsion and Political Reality.** Nehru projected the attainment of an interventionist state before the masses as an instrument for development and modernization. The state visualized by him had the potential to function with relative autonomy vis-à-vis the interests of the dominant class and the industrial and business groups. However, planned development became an essential instrument for patronage politics. The author argues that the programme of development and planning has become one of the ways by which the Congress established its dominance and the progressive expansion of its social base. The provision of affirmative action policies is a clear testimony to the government's commitment to the deprived sections of the society. He concludes that Nehruvian development is the product of both domestic compulsions and political realities of the nationalist movement and the subsequent post-independent era. However this policy of development has come under tremendous pressure in the era of globalization. The compulsions of political rationality had also affected the Nehruvian model of development. Indeed, both 'time' and 'space' influenced Nehru in moulding his model. It will be interesting to take stock of his perspectives in the neo-liberal context of the twenty first century.

1

Nehru, Mixed Economy and Aspects of Foreign Policy

A. K. Pasha

A couple of years ago , and even now, many people in high places denounced what India's first Prime Minister Jawaharlal Nehru stood for–mixed economy, planning, socialistic pattern of society, non-aligned movement, secularism, so on. Also, too much credit is being given to the economic reforms initiated since 1991. Nevertheless, India is seen as a major emerging economic power in Asia along with her military capability and political stability due to its strong commitment to democracy. [1]

One should briefly dwell on developments soon after Indian gained independence. The tragic events following the partition of the country presented major challenges to the government. The shortage of capital, need to rebuild the infrastructure and meet the growing demands of the people have to be considered. The challenge from Pakistan backed by the US on the Kashmir issue, cold war politics, Indian opposition to military alliances like Baghdad Pact [later CENTO], SEATO and others, Nehru's preference for rapid economic development were other factors. The Congress under Jawaharlal Nehru was cautious and so decided to go step by step from *Ramaraj* to the *Cooperative Commonwealth* and in the end to the *Socialistic Pattern of Society* and ultimately to *Socialism*. Nehru told the Avadi session of the Congress "We cannot have a welfare state in India with all the socialism or even communism in the world unless our national income goes up greatly. Socialism or communism might help you to divide your existing wealth, if you like, but in India there is no

existing wealth for you to divide, there is only poverty to
divide... how can we have a welfare state without wealth?"

For Nehru the Avadi Congress was a turning point closing
the earlier chapters of pre1947 hostility to socialism and post
1947 hesitation in plunging for that objective. Such a step by
step advance towards the socialist objective took the Congress
to a position in which it alone was capable of giving leadership
to the Indian people in their struggle for socialism. [2]
However in this connection the decision of the Indian National
Congress taken as early as in 1932 laid down the policy of
state control of basic industries or mother industries and
certain other essential industries or services was significant.
Nehru soon after adopting central planning in 1951 was
convinced that in India certain basic industries or the key
industries should be under state control, partly because he
viewed it to be "dangerous for those key and basic industries
to be controlled by private interests. [3] As for the other
industries, they can be under private control but when a state
plans its industrial or other development, planning itself
involves certain measure of control or direction from the state.
Otherwise as Nehru said, "there can be no planning. [4]

So the core industries or *commanding heights* came to be
identified as the public sector and this covered practically
major aspects of economy. Big river valley projects, dams,
steel plants, heavy machinery, coal, electricity generation and
distribution, airlines, tele-communications, transport, defence,
space, atomic energy, banking, pharmaceuticals, oil and gas,
railways, textile mills, education, universities, UGC so on.
Huge public sector companies like BHEL, ONGC, HAL,
HMT, IOC, BEL, ITI, AAI, ISRO so on came to be
established. At the moment there are 243 public enterprises.
Out of these are 103 textile mills which were nationalized by
Prime Minister Mrs. Indira Gandhi which are seen as a burden
on the economy. As early as in April 1953, Nehru said: "I shall
not rest content unless every man, women and children in the
country has a fair deal and has a minimum standard of living...

5 or 6 years is too short a time for judging a nation. Wait for another 10 years and you will see that our plans will change the entire picture of the country so completely that the world will be amazed". Reflecting the mood of the country, Nehru wrote in June 1955: "even though we have a multitude of problems and difficulties surround us and often appear to overwhelm, there is the air of hope in the country, a faith in our future and a certain reliance on the basic principles that have guided us thus far. There is the breath of the dawn, the feeling of the beginning of a new era in the long and checkered history of India. [5]

For Nehru the main problem before India was his desire to raise "standard of the masses, supply them with their needs, give them the wherewithal to lead a decent life and help them to progress and advance in life not only in regard to material things but in regard to cultural and spiritual things also. [6] Putting forward the social objectives of planning before the Parliament in 1954, Nehru had said: "We are starting planning for the 360 million human beings in India...what do the 360 million people want?...It is obvious enough that they want food; it is obvious enough that they want clothing, that they want shelter, that they want health... I suggest that the only policy that we should have in mind is that we have to work for the 360 million people; not for a few, not for a group, but the whole lot, and to bring them up on an equal basis. [7]

Producing goods and bringing about change was crucial and Nehru didn't give much importance to the *isms*. As he said: "In India, if we do not ultimately solve the basic problems of our country—the problems of food, clothing, housing so on–it will not matter whether we call ourselves capitalists, communists or anything else. The method need not belong to either of these two rival ideologies. It may be something in between. It may be that in India we may be able to find some way more suited to the conditions of our people, some middle way". He also said "I am not enamoured of these *isms* and my approach is, a pragmatic approach in considering the problem and I want to forget the *ism* attached to it. [8]

Nehru accepted the inevitability of private sector living side by side with the public sector which he was creating. In this connection Nehru as early as in 1954 wrote to Chief Ministers: "If India is to be really great, as we all want her to be, then she is not to be exclusive either internally or externally. She has to give up everything that is a barrier to growth in mind and spirit or in social life. [9] Nehru's open mind towards the private sector was quite visionary and shows his originality of thought. [10]

He believed in giving a "fair chance, a fair field and a fair profit" to the private industrialist. That is how Tatas, Birlas, Singhanias, Dalmia-Jains and others not only survived but prospered due to the expanding public sector. [11] For Nehru a welfare state and socialistic pattern of economy are not synonymous expressions? For him a socialistic economy must provide for a welfare state but it does not necessarily follow that a welfare state must also be based on a socialistic pattern of society. Therefore the two, although they overlap, are yet somewhat different, and he wanted both. For this to succeed from the very beginning the Nehru-Mahalanobis strategy of growth with equity had assumed that popular mobilization from below would be necessary to effectively implement radical measures in favour of the poor initiated by Nehru. [12]

While planning to establish the public sector economy, Nehru was conscious of the fact that India had to balance heavy industry, light industry, village industry and cottage industry. As he said: "We want heavy industry because without it we can never really be an independent country. Light industry too has become essential for us. So has cottage industry. [13] The view that Nehru neglected agriculture is not correct. He was well aware of the centrality of agricultural development in meeting his dream of rapid industrialization. The plan outlays on agriculture since the first plan were substantial. He placed great emphasis on creating the physical and scientific infrastructure necessary for modern agriculture.

Massive irrigation and power projects, numerous agricultural universities and research laboratories, fertilizer plants etc took their due place along with steel plant *as the temples of modern India* in the Nehruvian vision. As G.S. Bhalla says, "The qualitative technological transformation in India—the GR— came about not during his lifetime but soon after his death. But the foundations for the technological development were laid during Nehru's time. [14]

A foreign critic of Nehru saw mixed economy in this perspective: The main idea behind this system (which could be characterized as Soviet communism minus the violence but plus private property) were that Indians' scarce, inevitable resource needed to be directed to their socially most productive uses (including poverty alleviation and industrialization) and that only the government could be trusted to deploy capital efficiently to these ends – not the Indian market and certainly not the exploitative international market for goods and capital. [15]

Thus, Nehru's development strategy was based on three pillars: planning for industrial and agricultural growth, a Public Sector to develop strategic industries and a mixed economy. Nehru popularized the concept of planning and made it a part of Indian consciousness. India was to have a mixed economy as a transitional stage, with the private sector functioning for a long time to come though within the framework of planning. In the long run, the state was to occupy the commanding heights of the economy, owning or controlling all basic industries and strategic sectors of the economy. The Public Sector was not to be based only on state run enterprises. Nehru was very clear that the cooperative principle should be encouraged and cooperatives in trade, industry and agriculture should play an increasingly larger role. [16]

The three main basic features of mixed economy could be: (a) high degree of direct government ownership of industry; (b) high degree of government regulation of privately owned industrial businesses; and (c) the regulation of foreign trade (imports especially) and foreign investment. It must be pointed out that the real architect of mixed economy was the eminent engineer-statesman of Mysore, M. Visveswaraya, who published a volume under the title **Planned Economy for India** in 1936. This was full two decades before Nehru took the initiative to reorient India's planning process, earning for his exercise the name *socialist planning.* [17] In retrospect it's interesting to note that Nehru in the 1950's even at the peak of the cold war launched bold, imaginative forays into global diplomacy and made the world notice, admire and take poor, underdeveloped and emerging India seriously for its peace making qualities. His peace initiatives on the Korean crisis are noteworthy as the war was drifting dangerously in 1952 treating world peace. Nehru intervened at an appropriate time and proposed a neutral commission to oversee a sensitive POW's' repatriation and exchange between China and the USA. The 'Menon Resolution' was acceptable to the US but the Soviet Union and China were annoyed. India through this Menon proposal played a crucial role in stopping this war and India was soon appointed Chairman of the Neutral Nations Repatriation Commission.

For Nehru, foreign policy was closely linked to the country's economic policy and "until India has properly evolved her economic policy, her foreign policy will be rather vague, rather inchoate and will be groping. [18] Nehru in order to execute the economic policy he sought aid and assistance from the West but due his foreign policy stances, he could not get at the desired level. It was only the Soviet Union which helped India in her economic development especially industrialization. The cold war politics and US support to Pakistan became a stumbling block for US assistance. Like Japan, Taiwan, South Korea and even Thailand which got generous US aid and technical assistance, India had to rely primarily on Soviet help. [19]

The path of economic development that India chose based

on planning and a leading role for the Public sector in industrialization, especially in heavy industry brought her closer to USSR. While the Western powers, especially the US, hesitated to help, the Soviets readily came forward with assistance in the building of the Bhillai Steel Plant in 1956.Then followed the British in Durgapur and the Germans in Rourkela. The US was again approached for the Bokaro steel plant but when it continued to remain coy, the Soviets stepped in again. In the later years they played a critical role in oil exploration as well. In 1973-1974, it was established that "30 percent of India's steel, 35 percent of our oil, 20 percent of our electrical power, 65 percent of heavy electrical equipment and 85 percent of our heavy machine making machines are produced in projects set up with Soviet aid". Cold war politics and strong US-Pakistani ties and the stand of these countries had impacted Nehru's thinking with the result he repeatedly emphasized the need for self-reliance. This was because for Nehru "it is far better for us to fight in our own way than submit to them and lose all the ideals we have. [20] Due to 1962-65 wars and two successive drought years in 1965-66, food prices shot up and India was forced to import food grains in 1966.

During this period the US threatened to renege on commitments of food exports to India. The Indo-Pak war, India's stand on Vietnam and the desire to arm twist India into accepting an economic-policy package favoured by the US had convinced Johnson that India should be put *on a short leash* and what better way to do it than to cynically use India's desperate dependence on the US for food. India's decision to champion the cause of decolonization, support to National Liberation Movement's, opposition to colonial powers interventions like the Suez crisis (1956), and others became stumbling blocks. Nevertheless Nehru challenged US policies especially military alliances and bloc politics. As he very rightly said: "I do not think that anything could be more injurious to us from any point of view than for us to give up the policies that we have pursued, namely, those of standing up for certain ideals in regard to the oppressed nations and try to align ourselves with this great power or that and become its camp followers in the hope that some crumbs might fall from their table. [21]

Nehru vigorously championed the cause of the newly liberated countries of Asia and Africa from European colonialism. The Asian Relations Conference at New Delhi, the Bandung conference and his close friendship with Egypt's Nasser and Tito of Yugoslavia were some instances of his attempts to reach out to NAM states. As he said: "It is to the great advantage of India to try to attract to itself the sympathy and the hope of millions of people in the world without offending others. It is not our purpose to offend others or to come into conflict with others. [22] Although many have compared India with Yugoslavia, China, Russia, England, America so on but such comparisons may be helpful but they mislead. India has learned from the experiences from all these countries but the conditions in India are special and particular. Moreover India's background as Nehru noted, "Is in many ways peculiar, particularly the Gandhian background. [23] So Nehru's choices, preferences, Congress party's policies, cold war choices gave India limited access to economic and technical help. As Nehru asserted India "should not get help at the cost of our self respect. Then we are not respected by any party... we may get some petty benefits, but ultimately even these may be denied us. [24]

Many have also unjustly criticized Nehru for paying lip service to the principles of equality and socialism and that he acted at the behest of special interest lobbies representing the better–off. This may be unfair as his commitment to equitable distribution of income, high rate of tax and other stringent measures show his pro-poor approach towards the masses. [25] His commitment to the poor made him work for the mixed economy which in the long run, the role of the market forces and profit motive was to become less significant. At the same time, Nehru was quite clear that overtime the Public Sector must generate additional sources. According to the Industrial Policy Resolution of 1956, which he helped draft, the Public Sector was expected to 'augment the revenues of the state and provide resources for further development in fresh fields'.

Taking a pragmatic view of the question, he also held that where Public Sector performed well, it should remain, and where it did not, it was to be replaced. Above all Nehru wanted to build an independent self-reliant economy, for independence depended on economic strength and the capacity to resist economic and political domination. In achieving this, there is hardly any doubt that he was eminently successful. India did make the transition from a colonial to an independent economy. Whatever the weaknesses that emerged later, Nehru's economic policy did prove to be the right one for India and as a result her economic progress was quite remarkable. In the final analysis for Nehru external and internal affairs are closely interlinked hence his emphasis on secularism, communal peace and harmony. As he said: "Indeed, there is no basis for external affairs if internal affairs go wrong. [26]

Nehru set out to build an independent and self reliant economy and made an all out effort to break out of colonial underdevelopment and to ensure self sustaining and self-generating growth, both in agriculture and industry. No wonder he put a great deal of emphasis on self reliance and cautioned against dependence on other nations especially the West which had dragged its feet to transfer the technology India needed. Rapid industrialization, particularly growth of heavy industries, planning, development of the Public Sector, atomic energy and Science and Technology, technical modernization and the training of a large Technology and Scientific cadre were regarded by Nehru as necessary parts of the effort at independent economic development and self reliance. The biggest achievement he claimed for planning and for Congress rule was the creation of "a feeling of confidence....a feeling of self-reliance. [27] This he viewed would further strengthen national independence by increasing the self-confidence and self respect of the people. Nehru looked upon rapid economic development as basic for India's independence and unity and for the removal of poverty and implementation of his social policies. In the chapter on *Objectives of Planned Development*, which he wrote for the Third Five Year Plan he observed "A high rate of economic growth sustained over a long period is the essential condition for achieving a rising level of living for all citizens, and especially for those in low income groups or lacking the opportunity to work". [28]

One can compare India with Egypt for a variety of reasons. In July 1952 a fundamental change took place in Egypt with the overthrow of King Farook and the emergence of Gamal Abdel Nasser as the strongman of the new regime. This was an event of momentous significance for Egypt and a landmark in the history of the Arab World. It was to have far reaching consequences changing the very basic structure of the politics of the region. The new leaders decided to follow non-aligned foreign policy and opposed the Baghdad Pact in 1955. The Pact had divided the Arab world into two hostile camps: progressives and conservatives. By championing the Palestine cause, Nasser assumed the leadership of the Arab struggle against Israel. Nehru also criticized the Baghdad Pact and said it "has in fact created in West Asia far greater tension and conflict than every before. It has certainly put one country against another among countries that were friendly to one another". [29]

Nehru also saw the close association of the USA with the Baghdad Pact as an "unfriendly act toward India.....Taken with the Manila treaty the Baghdad Pact suggested that Pakistan had succeeded in encircling India with a ring of hostile alliances". [30] Both Nasser and Nehru came to have similar views on numerous global issues. Nehru sympathized with Arab nationalism represented by Nasser as the urge of the

Arab people. In supporting Nasser's Arab nationalism, Nehru cemented the ties between India and Egypt. Soon both India and Egypt began to move further towards each other impelled by forces within each other, but also by external factors. Egypt came to follow non-aligned policy abroad and secular policy at home. Nasser learnt the importance of planning and socialist pattern of society from Nehru. Identity of views between the two leaders brought the two states even more closely politically, economically and culturally. As a response to the Baghdad Pact, Egypt signed the Treaty of Friendship and Cooperation with India on April 5, 1955, which said: "There shall be perpetual peace, friendship and brotherly relations between India and Egypt and between their respective peoples". [31]

Nehru attached great importance to his friendship with Egypt as he viewed Cairo as the key to the success of India's policy towards the Muslim world and the Arab world in particular. However, it must be stressed here that Nehru urged Nasser and other Arabs not to rule out negotiations as a means of settling the Palestine issue. He also took care not to involve India too deeply in the dispute with Israel and at no time did he endorse the illogical claims of some Arab leaders. Nehru supported Nasser during the Suez crisis in 1956 when Britain, France and Israel attacked Egypt to regain Suez Canal and overthrow the regime of Nasser. Nehru publicly branded Israeli aggression as a case of "clear, naked aggression". [32]

'Peace-Keeping', which was an unknown term then, was invented to resolve the Suez war and India was part of that very first mission, the United Nations Emergency Force. Through his support to Nasser in the Suez crisis a much closer rapport between the two leaders was established. Whatever little sympathy was left for Israel in Nehru's heart vanished due to its aggression on Egypt and its alignment with Anglo French military action. Nehru concurred with Nasser on Israel, which was seen as an outpost of Western imperial interests and as a country that did not have any links in the area. Nehru attached great importance to his friendship with Egypt as he viewed Cairo as the key to the success of India's policy in the Arab world. He also saw this friendship as an example of India's stand as a secular country. He emphasized that both India and Egypt are the inheritors of two glorious and ancient civilizations. India sent several eminent Indians who were academics as ambassadors including AAA Fayzee who worked very hard to strengthen Indo-Arab cultural ties.

A cultural agreement was concluded in 1958 between Egypt and India and a chair of India studies in Cairo University was established. Indian Archaeology and history is also taught. Soon the flow of artists, writers, scholars, journalists, exchange of books, periodicals, films, music and dance groups, art shows, exhibitions and other types of cultural exchanges became common between India and all the Arab countries with whom India signed cultural exchange Programs. India's close ties with Egypt to a large extent neutralized the Pakistani offensive against India in the WANA region, especially over the Kashmir issue. Egypt went to the extent of declaring that Kashmir was an integral part of India and that "Suez is a dear to Egypt as Kashmir is to India: Pakistan was branded as the "number one enemy of Cairo and Arabs".

Pakistan's membership in the Baghdad Pact led to its isolation in the WANA region with even Saudi Arabia denouncing the Pakistani decision. In fact, Saudi Arabia's King Saud who had visited Pakistan in 1953 and extended Riyadh's' political support to Pakistan on the Kashmir issue was astonished to find that the "Islamic State of Pakistan should accede to those who have joined hands with the Zionist Jews" and called the Baghdad pact as a "stab in the heart of the Arab and Muslim states" and urged it *to return to the right path*, by withdrawing from the widely unpopular western military pact. Along with Egypt, Saudi Arabia also publicly sided with India over the issue of Indian Muslims. In a now famous public statement, the Saudi King proclaimed in December 1955; "I desire to say to my Muslim brethren all over the world with satisfaction that the fate of Indian Muslims is in safe hands". When Nehru visited Saudi Arabia in September 1956, he was given a rousing welcome with slogans of "welcome Prophet of Peace", which naturally angered Pakistani leaders. The Saudis were greatly impressed by Nehru's ideas for peace in Korea, Algeria, Turko-Greek tussle over Cyprus and in Vietnam. According to one writer all these interventions were not altruistic or purely moralistic but the objective was to raise India's stature as a peacemaker and an honest broker that does not carry the vested tag of superpowers. [33]

When Nehru in 1961 decided to take over Goa from Portuguese control, US Secretary of State JF Dulles issued a joint statement with the Foreign Minister of Portugal recognizing Goa as one of the 'Portuguese provinces' in Asia. "It overshadowed all the friendly assistance given by the US over the years and brought Indian feeling to a peak of anger." It was Nasser who prevented Portuguese and NATO ships from crossing the Suez Canal in 1961 on their way to Goa and greatly helped India. There was muted criticism from the NAM because the tremendous aura that India had in the 1950's was unmatched among developing countries during that period. [34]

The secession of Syria from the UAR in 1961, Egypt's military intervention in North Yemen after the 1962 revolution, US decision to supply offensive arms to Israel under Johnson, emergence of Faisal as Saudi King and his emphasis on Pan-Islamism to counter Nasser's Arab nationalism, all these were significant developments which made an impact on India's West Asia policy which had come to be identified as Cairo-centric. In order to contain Nasser, the US encouraged a Saudi-Iranian-Pak-Turkish alliance since 1964. Soon Riyadh termed India as an aggressor in the 1965 Indo-Pakistan war and warned New Delhi not to take undue advantage of its close ties with Arab and Muslim States. Egypt's defeat in the 1967 AIC and Nasser's death in

September 1970 at catapulted Riyadh the leading Arab State influencing the politics and foreign policies of several Arab states.

The Saudis under King Faisal quickly seized the opportunity by asserting their leadership in the area by reacting strongly to the damage done to the Al Aqsa mosque in Jerusalem (under Israeli occupation] the third holiest shrine of Islam, by arson on August 29, 1969, and calling for a conference of Islamic heads of state or government, which was held in Rabat (Morocco) on September 22-25, 1969. The Rabat summit paved the way for the establishment of the OIC in May 1971. For India the Rabat Islamic Conference gave a jolt to Indian diplomacy in the region. After having seen officially invited to participate in the conference at Saudi intervention, Pakistan staged a walk out from the Conference due to the presence of the Indian delegation led by Industries Minister Fakhruddin Ali Ahmed. This event evoked sharp criticism from several political parties in India towards Indira Gandhi's inept handling of the entire issue. For India it had become obvious that Pakistan would use the Islamic gatherings to denounce India and raise the Kashmir issue and plight of Indian Muslims, along with its declaration of World Islamic Solidarity. [35].

So far India in order to safeguard its interests in WANA extended support to the Palestinian Arab's and other Arab National Liberation Movement's in the area. India had come to establish close ties with secular nationalist regimes especially with Egypt under Nasser. India had also come to be friend, encourage and extend support to those countries, which opposed western sponsored military alliances like Baghdad Pact. India's friendship with Nasser and other progressive Arab leaders to some extent neutralized the Pakistani propaganda against India, especially over the Kashmir issue, as also during the 1965 Indo Pak war. Indian leaders were not only concerned about implications of developments in the region on India's security but also on its secular policy, which came to be appreciated gradually even by the so called conservatives in the WANA region. [36].

The Bangladesh crisis and the Indo-Pak war in 1971 had a major impact on India's ties with WANA, as Pakistan sought to get closer to the Arab States. With great skill India managed to convince the Saudi and other Arab/Muslim leaders about its desire to live in peace with Pakistan and respect its territorial integrity. The 1972 Shimla agreement and the release of Pakistani POW's helped the atmosphere as Saudi/Arab concern for Pakistan's integrity had become a major issue in India's bilateral ties. Moreover the new Egyptian President Anwar Sadat's preoccupation with the liberation of Sinai from Israeli occupation and his growing friendship with Riyadh, as also mounting differences with Moscow, constrained him to follow a policy of *neutrality* and *passive posture* towards India on the issue. Egypt's posture during the 1971 crisis in the sub continent brought home to India the harsh reality of little to choose between the so called progressive and conservative Arabs in their stand towards such a crucial issue affecting Indian security. In the light of new regional developments, India had to reorient its policy from one of heavy reliance on Cairo to other power centres, which had emerged in the region particularly Iraq, Algeria, Libya, Iran and the Arab Gulf monarchies. [37].

Israel's refusal to withdraw from occupied Arab lands compelled Egypt and Syria to launch a surprise military attack on Israel on October 6, 1973 who crossed the Suez Canal and the Golan Heights respectively. India supported the Arab military initiative. India declared that the cause of tension in the area "is due to Israeli aggression and refusal to vacate territories occupied by armed force. This intransigence on the part of Israel is clearly the basic cause leading to the present outbreak of hostilities. Our sympathies are entirely with the Arabs whose sufferings have long reached a point of explosion". India refused to call the Arab action as aggression. Justifying India's support to the Arab cause, it further said that the Arab cause was based on justice and demanded "immediate implementation by Israel of UN Security Council Resolution 242" for peaceful solution of the Arab Israeli Conflict [AIC]. Moreover, India's traditionally close ties with the Arabs required India to "stand by its friends in the time of their travail." [38]

Israel's refusal to withdraw from Arab lands made several of Israeli supporters abandon it just before and after the 1973 AIC and the subsequent oil embargo by OAPEC against USA and other supporters of Israel. India did not have to make such utterly opportunistic changes. The Arab states due to India's unequivocal support for the Arab and Palestinian causes assured New Delhi uninterrupted supply of oil and treated India as a *friend*. Thus, India due to its consistent support to the Arab causes managed to get assured oil supply. Moreover the above policy also opened significant possibilities for Indian exports. It also soon led to a large presence of Indian workers in the Gulf area. So far India's economic interaction was mainly concentrated with Egypt, Iran, Iraq and Sudan and at a low key with other Arab countries. But after the 1973 Arab–Israeli Conflict [AIC], India's economic and political contacts widened especially with the oil rich Gulf States. This partly alleviated India's balance of payment situation caused due to increase in oil prices. The outcome of the 1973 AIC conflict convinced Sadat that in the prevailing international situation a limited success in the war was the maximum that the Arabs could achieve and he visualized that only through diplomacy the AIC could be solved. He calculated that the US alone could compel Israel to vacate Arab lands, hence his famous saying that 99 percent of the cards in the AIC are with the US. This led him initially to conclude two disengagement agreements [DEA's] with Israel in 1974 and 1975. He visited Jerusalem on November 19, 1977 and concluded the Camp David accords in September 1978 and a bilateral peace treaty with Israel in March 1979 ending thirty years of armed confrontation with Israel. India's response to the Camp David accords was *uncritical but guarded.* [39]

In fact, New Delhi did not openly endorse or condemn the accords. Both Carter and Sadat sought India's support for the peace accords. The Indian Prime Minister Morarji Desai reminded both leaders that only a comprehensive solution would prove to be durable. Towards this end Desai felt Israel must withdraw from all Arab lands and Palestinians must be granted their just rights. He also underscored the need to resolve the issue of Jerusalem and Golan Heights. Shortly the Janata government extended qualified support to the accords saying that it "cannot but commend the efforts to bring about a peaceful solution to the problems of an area which has seen dangerous conflicts." [40]

One reason cited for the incoherent Indian response to the accords was the Egyptian factor. Although India wanted to steer clear out of any inter-Arab disputes, but New Delhi still valued friendship with Cairo and all efforts were directed towards preventing Egypt's isolation. No wonder India went to great lengths to prevent Egypt's expulsion or suspension from NAM, but could do nothing in OIC and Arab League. Earlier the emergence of the Janata Party in India after the defeat of Congress Party in 1977 elections raised the question of a review in India's West Asia policy. This was mainly due to AB Vajpayee of the Jan Sangh becoming the Minister of External Affairs who had been a vocal critic of India's support to the Arabs and who advocated close ties with Israel. It was during this period that Israeli Foreign Minister Moshe Dayan paid a secret visit in August 1977. But the Israeli leader achieved nothing concrete as Prime Minister Desai refused to establish ties with Israel unless the latter withdrew from all Arab lands. To the surprise of many but especially the US and Israel AB Vajpayee reiterated India's traditional policy towards the Arabs when he said: "there is no change in India's stand. Israel must vacate all occupied Arab territories and the legitimate rights of the Palestinian people must be restored." [41]

It must be recalled here that both India and Egypt started at the same time more or less. India became independent in 1947 and Egypt became really free in 1952. Both started planning process in early 1950's. Both fought similar number of wars- Egypt in 1948, 1956, 1967, 1973 with Israel and India –in 1948, 1962, 1965, 1971 with Pakistan and China. Both were friendly with Soviet Union and received economic, military and diplomatic support during the cold war. But Egypt under Sadat since at least 1974 identified closely with the USA and ended the armed confrontation with Israel in 1978 under the Camp David agreements. It became dependent on US economic and military aid and an ally and hence against the USSR. Although Egypt continued to profess non aligned policy but it's over dependence on the US became very obvious. After Sadat's assassination [which led Mrs. Indira Gandhi to comment that it's was due to his dependence on the US] Egypt lost interest in the Arab-Israeli conflict. When it did revive its interest the US and Israel ignored Egypt's initiatives. Egypt's muted response to Israeli invasions of Lebanon in 1978, 1982 and 2006 is a case in point. It has also facilitated US war on Iraq in 1991, UN sanctions on Iraq since 1990 and US invasion of Iraq in 2003. The US since 1973 and more especially since 1979 has entered the WANA region in a big way. The result is Egypt is largely seen as a client state of the US. India on the other hand strived to maintain its non aligned foreign policy with friendly relations with the Soviet Union until 1991 despite US support to Pakistan which created problems in Punjab, Kashmir, and North East India and all over India in general.

But India after the end of the cold war established diplomatic ties with Israel and worked hard to establish friendly ties with the US itself which emerged as the sole super power. But since the end of cold war and the reorientation in Indian foreign policy since then, US domination of West Asia especially in the Gulf region, renewed strategic ties between US-Pakistan in the new war on terror and developments in

Indo-US ties (June 2004 defence cooperation deal and 18 July 2005 nuclear deal) together with the Kashmir issues are developments which have impacted India's foreign policy. As Nehru said "We are potentially a great nation and a big power and possibly it is not liked by some people that anything should happen to strengthen us." [42] US domination, pre-emption and talk of uni-polar world are passing phases and the world is moving towards multi-polar world. One must reflect on what Nehru said many decades ago: "I think that not only in the long run, but also in the short run, independence of opinion and independence of action will count. [43] India's economy has been quite vibrant and its performance on the whole satisfactory. It has made long strides in almost all its different aspects. It has overcome economic-stagnation and broken through the vicious circle of poverty and underdevelopment. It has laid the foundations of a self-reliant, independent economy. It has thus fulfilled the design of the founders of the Republic, to go from political to economic independence. India's autonomous development has been free of subordination to the western economies. No longer has foreign capital had any stranglehold on Indian economy. The MNCs have played a minor role in Indian economy.

India successfully developed an economic pattern of its own, mixed economy, which placed equal emphasis on the active economic role of the state and the market and developed a complementary relationship between the public and private sectors. India has withstood the 1973 oil price hike, collapse of socialist economies [1991] with which India had close economic ties and the ASEAN economic [mainly financial] crisis of 1997. It was able to recover from 1991 fiscal crisis [during the Iraqi invasion of Kuwait] without serious dislocation. India has now entered a period of high economic growth and is on the way to becoming a major global economic power. The plans initiated by Nehru have now placed India as a leading power in the world.

But what Indian leaders since Nehru's death have more or

less ignored is the soft power–generating dynamo of peacemaking that Nehru did so ably even India's 'hard power' was limited. There are many conflicts like the Arab-Israeli, Iraq, Iran, Cyprus, Kurdish, and Afghan, Sri Lanka, Sudan so on where India's views will be *respected persuasive and imitable*. India established diplomatic relations with Israel in 1992 even though India recognized the Jewish state way back in 1950. The US and Israel persuaded India to take this step by assuring her that it can play a crucial role in the Madrid Arab–Israeli peace process, But the multilateral talks soon foundered and they collapsed as rapidly as they started. Again India was ignored when the 2003 Road Map for peace was unveiled to create an independent Palestinian state. "Throwing up hands and saying that Palestine or Sudan are outside India's core interest range will win no additional friends. If India can help break international logjams, credibility benefits would accrue. All it takes to offer pro bono peacemaking services is vision. Not a lot of material resources. Nehru commanded plenty of the former." [44]

Notes

1. Hiranmay Karlekar, ed., (1998) Independent India: The First Fifty Years, New Delhi, ICCR, OUP, pp.117-226, and 73-91.
2. EMS Namboodiripad, (1988) Nehru: Ideology and Practice, New Delhi, National Book Centre.
3. Jawaharlal Nehru's Speeches, Vol.1, 1946-49, New Delhi, Publication Division, 1983, 4th edition.p.142. Jawaharlal Nehru's Speeches, Vol.3, 1953-57, New Delhi, Publication Division, 1983, 3rd Edition.
4. Ibid. Jawaharlal Nehru, (1947), The Discovery of India, Calcutta, Signet Press.
5. Bipan Chandra et al., (2002) India after Independence, 1947-2000, New Delhi, Penguin Books, pp.131.
6. Jawaharlal Nehru's Speeches, (1983), Vol. I, 1946-49, Publication Division, 4th edition, New Delhi, p141.
7. Bipin Chandra et al., (2002) op cit., p. 500.
8. Nehru, op cit.140-141. Michael Breecher, (1959) Nehru: A Political Biography, Boston, Beacon Press.

9. Ibid., p.173.
10. Hiranmay Karlekar, (1998) op cit., p.135.
11. Nehru op cit., p.130. Jawaharlal Nehru, (1958) A Bunch of Old Letters, Bombay, pp. 304-305.
12. Bipin Chandra et al., (2002) op cit., p. 49.
13. Nehru, op cit., p. 19. Jawaharlal Nehru, (1949) Glimpses of World History, Vol.2, London, Lindsay Drummond.
14. Ibid., p.411-412.
15. Jim Rohwer, (1996) Asia Rising: Why America will prosper as Asia's Economies Boom, New York, Simon and Schuster, p.177.
16. Nehru, op cit., p.180.
17. EMS, Namboodripad (1988), op cit., p. 220.
18. Nehru, op cit., p.202. Sreeram Chaulia, *India's Soft Power: Lessons from Nehru.* Deccan Herald, March14, 2007.
19. Ibid., p.159. Jawaharlal Nehru, (1950) Independence and After: A Collection of Speeches, 1947-49, New York, pp. 202.
20. Ibid., p. 215.
21. Bipan Chandra et al., (2002) op cit., p. 214. Nehru, op cit., p.412-413.
22. Ibid., p. 218; The Hindu, February 12, 2004.
23. Ibid., p. 16.
24. Ibid., p. 219; M.S. Rajan, (1976) India's Foreign Relations During the Nehru Era, New Delhi, Asia Publishing House.
25. Ibid., p.180; Mohammed Heikal, (1973) The Cairo Documents, New York, pp. 278-279.
26. Ibid., p. 217. MS Agwani, *India and the Arab World*, in BR Nanda, ed., (1976) India Foreign Policy: The Nehru Years, New Delhi, pp. 66-77.
27. Ibid., p. 174. AK Pasha, (2004) *India and West Asia,* World Focus, Vol.25, October-December, pp. 41-46.
28. Ibid., p.179. MS Agwani, (1976) *Nehru and the Arab World*, Secular Democracy, Nehru Number, p. 171.
29. AK Pasha, (1990) *Nehru and the crises in West Asia,* Détente, Vol.9 no.1, May-June, pp. 4-9.
30. EMS Namboodiripad, (1988) op cit., p.216. AK Pasha, (1994) Egypt's Quest for Peace: Determinants and Implications, New Delhi, National Publishing House.
31. AK Pasha (1986), Egypt's Relations with the Soviet Union, the Nasser and Sadat Period, Aligarh, CWAS, AMU, pp. 9-10.

Sudha Rao, (1972) The Arab-Israeli Conflict: The Indian View, New Delhi, pp. 24-29.

32. AK Pasha, (1999) India and West Asia: Continuity and Change, Delhi, Gyan Sagar,; Nehru coordinated with the US on the Suez crisis and made many attempts to steer the war to an early end as India was one of the principal users of the Suez canal. US President Dwight Eisenhower discussed the possibility of setting up an *elder statesman board of appeals* composed of Nehru and himself to *develop a solution to the Arab-Israeli Conflict.* A joint Indo-US peace making effort was considered by the US as *commanding the respect of the world.* Sreeram Chaulia, *India's Soft Power: Lessons from Nehru.* Deccan Herald, March, 14, 2007.

33. AK Pasha, (1995) India and OIC: Strategy and Diplomacy, New Delhi, Centre for Peace Studies.

34. EMS Namboodiripad, (1988) op cit., p. 216. AK Pasha, (1991) *Indo-Egyptian Ties: Retrospect and Prospects*, Third World Impact, Vol. 2, no. 20/23, pp. 23-27. AK Pasha, *Rediscovering old Bonds with Egypt*, The Pioneer, 23 December 1991. Hari Sharan Chhabra, (1989), Nehru and Resurgent Africa, New Delhi, Africa Publications, pp. 44-51, and 33-39.

35. AK Pasha, ed., (1999) Perspectives on India and the Gulf States, New Delhi, Détente Publications.

36. AK Pasha, ed., (1999) Contemporary Gulf: State, Society, Economy and Foreign Policy, New Delhi, Détente Publications, pp. 1-28.

37. AK Pasha, *India and West Asia: Continuity and Change,* in Nalini Kant Jha, ed., (2000) India's Foreign Policy in a Changing World: Essays in Honour of Professor Bimal Prasad, New Delhi, South Asian Publishers, pp. 240-269.

38. AK Pasha, *India and West Asia,* World Focus, Vol. 25, October-December 2004, pp. 41-46.

39. AK Pasha, ed., (2000) Arab-Israeli Peace Process: An Indian Perspective, New Delhi, Manas.

40. AK Pasha, *India's Cultural Diplomacy in West Asia and Indo-Egyptian Relations* In AK Sinha and AK Singh eds. (2007), Udayana: New Horizons in History, Classics and Intercultural Studies, Delhi, Anamika Publications, pp. 295-310.

41. Nejma Heptullah, (1991) Indo-West Asian Relations: The Nehru Era, New Delhi, Allied.

42. Nehru, op cit., p 221. AB Sawant, *Nehru's Perception of Foreign policy*, South Asian Studies, Vol. 29, no. 2, July-December, 1994, pp. 92-96.
43. Ibid., p. 218.
44. Bipan Chandra et al., (2002), op cit., p. 496. Sreeram Chaulia, *India's Soft Power: Lessons from Nehru*. Deccan Herald, March 14 2007. *Call for Decentralization of Power in Centre-State ties,* The Hindu, Thiruvananthapuram, July 7 2006.

2

From Nehru to *Pravasi Bharatiya Diwas*: Changing Contours of India's Diaspora Policy

Aparajita Gangopadhyay

This paper [1] presents aspects of continuity and change in India's policy towards its diaspora. While distilling half a century of reflections on the subject - from the Nehru era right down to the UPA (United Progressive Alliance) regime - it particularly focuses on historical development of India's policy towards its diaspora beginning with Jawaharlal Nehru to the recent initiatives undertaken by the government such as the celebration of Prawasi Bharatiya Diwas and the creation of a separate Ministry for Overseas Indians in the light of the recommendations of the L.M. Singhvi Report. The primary objective is to understand the implications of these initiatives vis-à-vis noticeable 'shifts' in the foreign policy matrix of the Indian state.

As is well-known, the policy adopted by Jawaharlal Nehru, after Independence in 1947, considered the overseas Indians as an external entity outside the purview of Indian domestic and foreign policy formulations. Nehru categorically advised his overseas brethren to integrate themselves within their host countries. This policy of impassiveness towards the expatriate Indians continued till the 1980s. Thereafter, a slow but steady transformation seems to have been set in motion so far as policy towards Indian Diaspora is concerned. The submission of the L.M. Singhvi Committee Report on People of Indian Origin (PIOs) and Non-Resident Indians (NRIs) (on 8 January 2002) may be looked at as the most important embodiment of this change in outlook and approach. Even though the Report was submitted during the NDA rule, there is as yet no evidence to suggest that the present UPA Government has any reservations on this count. In fact, the celebrations of the Fifth Pravasi Bharatiya Divas held in Delhi on 7-9 January 2007, testifies to certain continuity in policy terms.

The paper is divided into three broad sections, essentially chronological slices of post-independence trajectory of Indian nation state. In Section I, an overview of the diaspora policy of Nehru is analysed. Section II deals with an overview of the diasporic policy post-Nehru to the early initiatives during the liberalization period taken by the Indian government till the mid-1990s. Finally, the last section deals with the 'shifts' in the governmental position under the BJP leadership, the subsequent Singhvi report, the continuity of policies by the UPA.

Antecedents of the Indian Diaspora

The Indian diaspora is one of the largest diasporas in the world, with its presence in all continents. In many of the countries the people of Indian origin form one of the largest ethnic groups, like in Fiji, Mauritius, Suriname, Trinidad and Tobago, Guyana and Nepal. The immigration of these people to overseas was in two distinct phases: a) overseas emigration in the nineteenth and the early part of twentieth century or emigration during the colonial period; b) twentieth century migration to the industrially developed countries or emigration in post-colonial period. The first phase of this emigration in the nineteenth and the twentieth century witnessed the unprecedented emigration of indentured and other labourers, traders and professionals and employees to the British, French and the Dutch colonies in Asia, Africa and Latin America. In the colonial period, broadly three distinct patterns of Indian emigration were identifiable: (1) "indentured" labour emigration, [2] (2) Kangani and maistry labour emigration, [3] and (3) "passage" or "free" emigration. [4] The colonial government officially sponsored the indentured labour emigration, named after the contract 3 signed by the individual labourer to work on plantations. It began in 1834 and ended in 1920. The indentured labour was essentially taken to British Guiana, Fiji, Trinidad and Tobago, Jamaica, and to the French colonies of Guadalupe and Martinique, and the Dutch colony of Suriname. The second type of emigration was essentially to Ceylon, Malaya and Burma. Thirdly, those who paid their passage moved to South and East Africa. In contrast, during the second phase of migration, mainly professionals moved to the industrialised nations of the west as part of what is referred to as *brain drain*.

During the first phase of migration, the colonial management was to be the *protector* of these immigrants and would take care of their welfare. It was only in the early part of the twentieth century that some voices within the freedom movement in India criticised the fate of the indentured labour to the British and other European colonies. For example, the Indian freedom movement recognised the demands of the Indians living in British East Africa for equality within the races, political representation, rural landownership and urban residence. [5] Many Indian leaders cited the unscrupulous ways of labour recruitment - by fraud and by force-and the treatment meted to them, both during the long journeys and in plantations, and called it as *a system of slavery in disguise*. [6] Despite the voices raised by freedom fighters in India against the indenture system, the practice was carried out unabated till January 1, 1920. [7]

The British encouraged the indentured labour to settle down in their island (especially in Fiji, Mauritius, Trinidad and Tobago) colonies following the ban on indenture system to serve essentially the interest of British plantations. Moreover, the British position was that the Indians were simply citizens of whatever colony they lived in. When later India applied to appoint agents in the West Indies and Fiji to help monitor the grievances of the diaspora, the colonial office refused on grounds that the Indians were permanent residents 'enjoying harmonious relations with the other sections of the local populations'. For instance, in 1923 L.B. Shastri appealed against the colour bar in colonies but the British did not pay heed to this appeal. The 38th Indian National Congress Annual Session in December 1923 declared that unless India became independent, the grievances of the Indian diaspora could not be properly remedied. [8] As a result, with the independence of most of these former colonies, a legacy of hatred between the descendents of emancipated African slaves and the Indian indentured labour emerged. With the independence of India, the newly independent state had to come to terms with its former colonial master and the Indians living mostly in the former British Commonwealth.

Diaspora at a Distance: The Nehru Years

India was in a dilemma when it came to the expatriate Indians living aboard after 1947. India's foreign policy formulator Jawaharlal Nehru felt that India's foreign policy dictated independence from all foreign involvement, with its focus on Non-Alignment and good relations with the developed as well as the developing nations (especially the newly emerging Asian and African countries), and excluded a specific policy towards the overseas Indian community. Nehru had *made the expatriate Asians alien in a legal sense* and their status did not allow for any special relationship between them and the Indian state. [9] In order to put India in the world map and seek the acceptable of other nations of India's independence, Nehru could do so in two ways: either by the utilisation of force or by gaining of respect and moral authority. Nehru wanted to use the latter to do so. M.C. Lall asserts that thus, the Nehruvian model had three components— rhetorical, emulative and mediatory. [10] It was the only rational option for Nehru to seek the friendship of the newly independent countries of Asia and Africa by aiming to "create a larger area of peace by fighting common dangers of imperialism and racism together". [11]

Nehru had made the expatriate Asians aliens in the legal sense and the status did not allow for any special relationship between them and the Indian state. This position had several drawbacks—India could not get involved when part of the diaspora was going through political, economic and social discrimination or even a severe crisis. Despite the continuing informal ties, which remained between the members of the diaspora and their families in the place of their origin, they were not encouraged to take part in the economic development of India. Nehru had followed a highly moralistic policy during the national struggle, which now spilled over to independent India making a conscious nation state project to exclude the diaspora.

For the larger goal of newly emergent Asian-African solidarity, India adopted a cultivated apathy towards its diaspora. Nehru's policy was to a certain extent also linked to the fact that all problems concerning the diaspora were no loner inter-imperial matters to be solved under the auspices of one great regulatory power. India could not afford to be vociferous on the fate of the Indians abroad and put potential good diplomatic relations at risk. Although, for instance for almost 15 years, India provided under the special commonwealth assistance programme, 1500 training places for nationals from a number of African nations, from Ghana to Kenya, Tanzania to Zanzibar. [12] Many doctors, engineers, experts, teachers and others trained under this programme. But India made no deliberate move to use the people of Indian origin for the purpose of negotiations with the African and Asian nations. Lall says that, "India became supportive of Africanisation even to the detriment of Indian settlers". [13] This policy had several limitations. India did not get involved fearing spoiling its relations with the newly decolonised world and did not even take up the issue of violation of human rights there. [14] On the other hand, Bhiku Parekh says although overseas Indians took considerable interest in India they did not develop a tradition of discourse on it comparable to those of the Jewish, English, Irish and other diasporas about their respective homelands. The perceptions of the overseas Indians who went in pre-colonial times about their homeland was largely nostalgic, sentimental, patchy and without a focus. [15]

While the diasporic discourse on India was acquiring a clear and coherent character, the same cannot be said about the Indian discourse on diaspora. As India took little interest in overseas Indians, the past protestations of the plight of the indentured labourers and their terms of employment were soon forgotten. After independence successive Indian governments adopted an attitude of studied indifference to the overseas Indians lest they should appear to be interfering in the internal affairs of another country. They were anxious not to appear as their protector, or to encourage their return back to India, nor to expose them to the suspicion of divided loyalty. [16]

The Government of India pushed for the expatriates to integrate with the society of their host country. This was partly out of concern for independent India's new diplomatic overtures towards the newly decolonising world. Moreover, it was a strong belief in India that the expatriate Indians had become part of the controlling category in many of these former colonies, and in order to maintain their privileged position through their control of the country's economy had adopted the discriminatory policies like their colonial masters towards the public. In Africa, it was observed that while the British imperial system had kept the different racial groups separate, the Indians too had shown no inclination to integrate with the African masses and support them in their struggle for independence.

Nehru had been clear in enunciating his foreign policy goals that plainly stated that the Indians who had left their country of origin to seek employment abroad had to integrate with the local population, support their struggles for freedom, and even put 'their cause first'.

It is the consistent policy of the government that persons of Indian origin who have taken foreign nationality should identify themselves with and integrate in the mainstream of social and political life of the country of their domicile. The government remains naturally alive to their interests and general welfare and encourages cultural contacts with them. As far as Indian citizens residing abroad are concerned, they are the responsibility of the Government of India. [17]

He pointed to their economic success in these countries where they were guests, and stated that it was their turn to support their movements of political struggles. In the Lok Sabha he stated: "Now these Indians abroad, what they are? Indian citizens! Are they going to be citizens of India or not? If they are not, then our interest in them becomes cultural and humanitarian, not political...Either they get the franchise as nationals of the other country, or treat them as Indians minus the franchise and ask for the most favoured treatment given to an alien". [18] The Government of India for almost four decades followed the Nehruvian policy. Indians aboard were advised to accept local citizenship and cease to separate their future from those of the local people. Therefore, Sunil Khilnani in his book *The Idea of India* writes: "...Nehru believed that an Indian identity could emerge only within the territorial and institutional frame of a state". [19] Accordingly Anirudh Gupta writes, "The Nehru policy was based on the unrealistic hope that within the broad pattern of African-Asian nationalism the separate identity of Indian immigrants would be forgotten". [20] It was felt that if India championed the cause of its émigrés too vociferously the matter could cause diplomatic problems between two sovereign states. Moreover, India needed the support of these countries to fight against a larger imperialist policy worldwide.

Therefore, independence hardly brought any anticipated relief to the plight of overseas Indians in the British and French colonies as a consequence of the distinct Nehruvian policies of respecting national sovereignties, cultivating amicable international relations, non-interference into the affairs of other nations and the pursuit of non-alignment.

According to Bhiku Parekh, "The Indian lack of interest in overseas Indians had also its roots in its patronising attitude to them. For the politically minded Indians, including Nehru and the socialists, overseas Indians were either poor or illiterate and this was a liability, or they were rich men who exploited the local population and thereby an embarrassment". [21] Many Indians also felt that overseas Indians had developed a habit of clinging on to India, as a result neither did they integrate with the natives nor evolved an autonomous life of their own.

Revisiting the Diaspora: A Studied Ambivalence to Liberalisation

Till the 1970s there existed a separate department concerned with the overseas Indian affairs located within the Ministry of External Affairs, but most of its work remained classified. According to Srikant Dutt, "It seems to be impossible to get any exact information on this particular department; it was most probably linked to the movement to stop the brain drain, which was being noticed at that time". [22] For example, Indira Gandhi was particularly interested in reclaiming Indian scientists to help in Indian development. On the other hand, she made herself unpopular during the East African crisis of 1968-72 when she endorsed the Nehruvian policy of non-interference and stressed on India's relations with the African nations first over her concern for the treatment meted out to the Indians there. It was only in the South African case that economic and political sanctions were taken up to further the cause of the Indian community there.

Another reason for the pursuit of this policy was the issue of citizenship. Although the Constitution of India under Article 8 provided citizenship for the children of those whose parent or grandparent was born in India, the issue of dual citizenship was never raised because of the question of loyalty. But those who wished to return could get back their citizenship, but there were a number of associated complications. Therefore,

Nehru's Republic Day addresses in 1960-62 of the 'mother country' and the position of the overseas Indians as ambassadors to the host countries was duly accepted. So it became part of India's policy when it became supportive of the decolonisation in Asia and Africa, leaving the diaspora to fend for it. According to Lall, "What the Government of India did not want were split loyalties among those living in one country, holding the passport of the second and investing in a third, all out of reasons of security or convenience". [23] Moreover, Indian Citizenship Act explicitly abolished dual nationality under the Constitution between 1947 and 1955; the matter of dual nationality still remained somewhat vague. [24] The Indian Citizenship Act was redrafted in 1955 cleared all ambiguities. The Act now made no difference between the Commonwealth states and other states and the Act was universally applicable to all.

The expatriate Indians became aliens like any other foreigners and the Government of India (GOI) restricted their rights in buying/owning property and investing in their country of origin. With the Janata government's advent to power in 1977, some significant changes in the policy were being considered. Some changes envisaged included rectification in the laws that would permit Indians living overseas to their 'motherland', even if they were foreign nationals. The government also organised a seminar and declared that the Indian Council of Cultural Relations would be involved with the Indian diaspora. They reiterated that the Indian foreign policy would try and attain the right balance between pursuing its diplomatic goals and the issues concerning the overseas Indians.

The first time any mention of a special department or agency was in 1986, when a special approval committee was constituted within the department of Industrial Development for the expeditious clearance of the industrial proposals of NRIs (Non-Resident Indians). Then in 1987, an Indo-NRI Chamber of Commerce and Culture was set up to promote the overseas Indians' cases [25] making it clear that the Government of India in reality did not have a central machinery to deal with the expatriates till the mid 1980s. The changes were evident especially in the areas of buying properties between aliens and the NRIs. The latter were allowed to purchase properties in specified areas, with strict rules and regulations extended to all such NRIs. These measures were the result of an early phase of liberalisation in the 1980s. The GOI hoped would fuel back some investments into the country, yet the procedures reeked of 'red-tapism' that kept the NRIs out.

There were several reasons for the transformation in the attitude of the Indian government towards the overseas expatriates. Firstly, stereotypes were broken as more Indians came in contact with the overseas expatriates. This also led to a sense of "pride in their struggles and achievements, a desire to reciprocate their affection, and a sense of guilt for having neglected them for so long". [26] Secondly, India's self interest also played a vital role. India's foreign exchange situation was worsening from the 1970s and the Indians who had moved out after the independence into the developed countries were successful and prosperous. India looked towards them for not only "remittances but also by their technological, scientific, managerial and other skills". [27] Overseas Indians now became extremely important and were given the status of NRIs that 'reduced their diasporic existence to a matter of mere residence'. [28] The Nehruvian policy continued till the early 1990s with two significant changes: the foreign policy priorities changed from a global, ideological to a regional and more realistic one (from Nehru to Rajiv Gandhi) and then a change in foreign economic policy from a closed economy to a relatively open one (Rajiv Gandhi to PV Narasimha Rao). [29]

But by 1991 the end of Cold War had brought significant transformations globally, and India had to face new political, economic and security challenges. India too was aware of the many 'other Indians' in the world by this time, and within India there began a debate about the expatriate Indians living in these countries. Additionally, the economic woes of India too had increased by 1991 and its foreign exchange reserves had reached an all time low. India's import bills on oil too have risen sharply as a consequence of the Gulf War.

In addition, there had been a change in composition and class of those moving overseas from the colonial period to the period of post-independence. The latter emigration was taking place essentially to the west and to the Gulf countries. From those living in the Gulf the remittances were high, and those moving out as part of the 'brain drain' kept informal ties with their mother country. The Gulf labourers remained different from the migrants to the West. Throughout the period of the 1970s to 1990s the Indian members of parliament raised questions about the welfare of those Indians living in the Gulf. Indian government also subsequently signed a number of treaties with various Gulf governments on issues such as deportations, labour laws, as well as a change in its own Emigration Act in 1983. The Gulf War also witnessed the work of the Special Coordination Unit and the Overseas Indians Division in evacuation of the Indians working in there. [30] The term NRI first appears in the parliamentary debates in 1984, but did not replace the other headings in the indexes of 'Indians abroad' or the 'People of Indian Origin' or even the 'expatriate Indians'. There is moreover, no clear delimitation to who was a NRI and who was not till 1991, when the definition was linked to citizenship.

The Narasimha Rao Government embarked on a New Economic Policy that called for immediate and extensive reforms. The economy was for the first time opened up to outside investors who could acquire a majority share holding in the Indian companies. A plan to dismantle the public sector loss making units was also decided upon. Subsequently, the tariffs were slashed and the rupee was made convertible on the trade account. Thereafter, the rupee was also devalued. The

Minister of State of the Finance Ministry R. Thakur stated that: "...the resulting improvement in our balance of payments will restore the confidence of the NRIs in the Indian economy and encourage the inflow of foreign exchange from the NRI sources". [31]

There were a number of special concessions for the NRIs to invest in the Indian industries, and set up new industrial ventures or deposit their foreign currency in the Indian banks. [32] Despite these relaxations there remained the blockades associated with the repatriation of the profits, alongside the overwhelming bureaucratic hurdles. The pre-1991 economic crisis had also seen the opposition parties also speaking up for the cause of the NRIs and portraying them as the 'saviours of their mother country'. But the Congress government in power clearly stated that they did not feel that the NRIs would simply move their money into the country out of sheer patriotism. The government also strongly felt that the investments were required in form of joint ventures instead of deposits in the banks that could leave the country without a moment's notice. The strong feeling that persisted among large sections within the government was that the money lend by the NRIs would be a debt that could lead India to default on payments later.

Therefore, the subsequent failures of the government to speed up the reforms made the rhetoric of attracting the NRIs seem empty. The policy implementation was slower than the political declarations of the government. Many parties opposed this liberalisation and criticised the government on the grounds that these reforms did not reach the masses. The breakaway from the Nehruvian tradition did not happen quickly enough. The government continued to drag its feet and the loss making PSUs continued to function. Three main reasons could be cited for the disinterest of the NRIs in the Indian economy, reasons both institutional and historical. Firstly, India's colonial past had made her mistrust any investment that came from abroad. The 'ideological legacies' made her move towards development and planning associated with the public sector.

Secondly, the bureaucracy that had ruled the country since 1947, was based on the 'license raj or the permit raj'. The 1991 reforms changed little of the bureaucracy as heavy regulation remained in place and the public sector continued to exist. Finally, the strong opposition that was offered by the local industrialists who were not in favour of removing the 'protection' that they had enjoyed over the years, and face challenges from the outside competitors that would snatch away the long monopolies. Therefore, there were many political enunciations minus a real political will. [33]

At the same time, the NRIs also placed their demands for a bail out plan of the Indian economy. They wanted the reforms to go all the way to protect their investments and use them efficiently. The question of dual nationality also arose. The NRIs felt that granting Indian citizenship would make investing in India easier, as under the present rules they could not stay in India for more than 180 days. Confusion prevailed within various circles of the government and the press as contradictory statements were made by a large number of government officials. For example, Eduardo Faleiro, the Minister of State for External affairs declared in 1991 that the government was considering dual citizenship, whereas some others stated that it was not possible. This uncertainty ended when the Minister of State for Parliamentary Affairs and Home Affairs, M.M. Jacob stated: "The concept of dual citizenship is not consistent with the Constitution of India and Citizenship Act, 1955...citizenship was not clearly defined before the passage of the Independence of India Act". [34] In fact, the government was of the view that such a step would be hazardous to national security as Pakistani citizens could in effect claim Indian citizenship. [35]

Moreover, the idea of representation in the Lok Sabha was voted out as the parliamentarians felt that the NRIs would take over their constituencies and buy the votes with their money. Besides, some sections also highlighted the lack of 'morals' of the NRIs and their bad effect in the country. Lall, quotes N. H.

Khan, who highlights the NRIs disinclinations due to: "Once here, they come up against business partners who fleece them of their money, land deals that often turn out to be fraudulent, arrogant bureaucrats, corrupt officials and red tape. Multinational companies have a system of PR agencies to deal with these kinds of blocks. But for the individual NRI, the signal reads: You are not welcome". [36]

Accordingly Lall states that the NRIs being a 'hidden asset' in terms of economic potential did not strike the Indian government till the 1990s. Even after liberalisation and the public realisation that the diaspora could lift India out of the economic problems that she was facing, there was little the government was prepared to do to establish a relationship in order to cash in on the asset. [37] She calls the relations between India and the NRIs a case of 'mutual abandonment'. Therefore, mistrust continued between the government and the NRIs. It was felt that the government of India had shown disregard towards the expatriates, and its inability create the right economic environment was the cause of the estrangement between India and her diaspora. In the past, only on two occasions had the Indian government had asked the expatriates to contribute towards the defence efforts in the disputes with Pakistan and China.

All this made it clear that now India was targeting towards it's expatriates who had left in the post-Independence period mostly to the developed countries of the West for any economic pull-off. The NRI, therefore, became synonymous with that Indian who had moved towards the West to improve his economic status, and not those who left the country as indentured labour, petty traders or those who paid for their passage especially under the colonial rule. The latter group was no longer the focus of interest as far as the economic priorities were concerned. Bhiku Parekh cites two reasons for India's new-found interest in its diaspora. He says that the attention towards the older diaspora was largely cultural, patchy and patronising. The concern with the immigrations to the West was largely economic and political, intended to attract their capital and skills, and further to mobilise their political influence. The latter much pampered group enjoys undue public attention in India. [38] Similarly, Mahim Gosine says that India's perception of east Indians who lived in the societies of diaspora is negative. [39]

Among other reasons cited, Davesh Kapur states that the prevailing wisdom in India until recently paid little attention to international trade. As a result the importance of overseas trade networks provided by its diaspora was underplayed.

This became an important reason why Indians in East Africa and Hong Kong were not courted by the Indian government and Indian business despite the potential pay offs. India's fears of the outside World were reflected not just in its policies towards international trade and FDI but also an apathy bordering on resentment towards its more successful diaspora. [40]

In the last decade, the transformation of the ideological climate in India and the success of the diaspora, especially in the US, have instilled much greater self-confidence in both. The resulting lack of defensiveness has been an important reason for the growing links and stronger bonds, which have transformed relations between Indian and its diaspora.

The 'New' Diaspora Policy

The advent of BJP through the NDA brought about a radical shift in the policy of the government of India. They quickened the pace of the reforms and speeded up the move towards integration with the process of globalisation. They recognised that the technology transfers and the augmentation of the foreign exchange reserves were part of its New Industrial Policy. The BJP government took the entire process of liberalisation ahead that had been stated by its predecessor, the Congress. [41] The NRIs were in greater focus, as they were encouraged even more than before to invest in India, with general relaxations across the board for them. A special proposal for NRIs was announced with the launching of the People of Indian Origin Card Scheme on 31 March 1999. The PIO card allowed for some special economic, educational, financial and cultural benefits besides acting as a long-term visa for the cost of US$ 1000 for the duration of 20 years. [42] This shift was clearly evident by 1999, when the Chennai Declaration of the BJP included:

We believe that the vast community of NRIs and PIOs also constitute a part of the Great Indian Family. We should endeavour to continually strengthen their social, cultural, economic and emotional ties with their mother country. They are the rich reservoir of intellectual, managerial and entrepreneurial resources. The Government should devise innovative schemes to facilitate the investment of these resources for India's all–around development". [43]

In September 2000, the Government constituted a High Level Committee on Indian Diaspora in under L.M. Singhvi to look into the matters concerning the NRIs and the People of Indian Origin. The Government of India Committee on the Indian Diaspora was created to recommend a broad and flexible policy framework after reviewing the status, needs and role of persons of Indian origin (PIOs) and non-resident Indians (NRIs). The Committee was headed by L M Singhvi, MP (BJP) and former High Commissioner to Britain, with the rank of a cabinet minister, and submitted its report by 7 December 2001 to the Minister of External Affairs. The Committee looked at the role of PIOs and NRIs in India, the rights and facilities extended to them, and also examined the conditions of their existence including their rights discrimination in the countries of their residence. [44] Although, the PIO card was announced, still in 1999 and 2000 budgets the NRIs were hardly mentioned at all.

The Singhvi Committee Report is the latest input concerning the rethinking of the diaspora issue by the BJP government. The Prime Minster Atal Behari Vajpayee released the Singhvi Report on January 8, 2002. The Report is

structured in five parts. [45] Prime Minister Atal Behari
Vajpayee stated: "We are in favour of dual citizenship but not
dual loyalty. The loyalty with India will remain but they will
also be loyal to the country where they have taken citizenship
but it has been resolved now. I am hopeful that Indians settled
abroad will find it suitable". [46] The dual citizenship will be
applicable to people of Indian origins living in 7 countries-US,
UK, Canada, Australia, New Zealand, a large part of Europe
and Singapore. [47] The issue of dual citizenship has emerged
as the most controversial in the report. Commenting on the
idea of dual citizenship Jayati Ghosh writes in the *Frontline*
that: "The government's apparent intentions on the issue of
dual citizenship make it clear that certain elite Non-Resident
Indians are to be treated differently from ordinary Indian
citizens, both at home and abroad". [48]

The dual citizenship according to Ghosh could provide
advantages in two areas, as those NRIs who are part of the
PIOs are given special incentives for investment in India.
These benefits could be, firstly, ownership of various forms of
property within the country and participation in the electoral
processes, both through voting and contesting in the elections.
Moreover, those who have migrated to these countries belong
to the professional classes and would like to remain part of the
decision making process. The inherent bias is visible as all
PIOs are not eligible for the dual citizenship. For example,
such privileges will not be granted to those who are the
descendents of the indentured labour in the Caribbean or in Fiji
or those who are in Africa, whose ancestors went as petty
traders. These people's lack of political connections through
extended families as well as the financial contributions will
make them incapable of applying for the dual citizenship.
Therefore, by granting them *dual citizenship* these 'NRIs' will
benefit greatly. They can then enjoy the material benefits of
the west as well as simultaneously take advantage of the
political rights and decision-making capacities back in India.
[49]

What more, the declarations by the various governments in the last five decades that granting of dual citizenship will be endangering the state's security and that the Citizenship Act does not permit this seems to have been lost. The issue of loyalty to one country, which had been the crux of matter in the past, seems also to have become irrelevant. In that context, the PM's statement as well as that of L.M. Singhvi create certain confusions and contradictions—Will the dual citizenship need an amendment to the Citizenship Act of 1955 or not? It is also clear that the expectation about bailing India out by the NRIs does not seem to hold water, as their responses continue to remain lukewarm at the best. The NRIs continue to have strong familial and kinship relations with India but are not interested to invest here.

The aim at wooing the Indian diaspora in the western countries could be seen as part of that dramatic shift in India's policy since 1997. If one can stretch this argument that by providing the diasporic Indians these inducements they hope to inculcate and develop within the Indian diaspora a strong pro-India lobby in these countries that could help India back home. These countries could then look at India more favourably for investments as well as be more positive towards India's foreign policy posturing (like creation of a strong India caucus). The Indians living there are rich and have substantial financial clout. Mr. Singhvi stressed for the need for rethinking in India of its diaspora because of current changes in society and economy that had tremendous implications for the Indian diaspora. He stated that Indians operated in a web of relationships and the networked economy held tremendous possibilities for the prosperity of the Indian Diaspora (like China). [50]

As a continuation of the policy to attract the NRIs the subsequent Pravasi Bharatiya Diwas (PBD) have given out attractive sops to the diaspora. For instance during the third PBD, the President A P J Abdul Kalam called the NRIs to fund the establishment of an Overseas Indian Research Foundation

(OISF) to support research in challenging areas including earthquake prediction and involve themselves in extending urban amenities to rural areas of the country. He also called upon the Indian diaspora to consider establishing "PURAs (Providing Urban Amenities in Rural Areas)" in order to deal with the mammoth challenges faced by India. The Prime Minister Dr. Manmohan Singh during the next PBD launched the Overseas Citizens of India (OCI) scheme that granted a life-long multiple entry visa. He further announced that the government would extend dual citizenship to all overseas Indians who had migrated out of the country after 26 January 1950. During the fifth PBD the government announced that it was examining a proposal to establish an Indian Overseas Facilitation Centre that would offer investment advisory services for investors. Also the government would be examining the proposal to establish an university for Persons of Indians Origin. [51]

Conclusion

One can discern three major shifts in India's policy orientation towards its diaspora since independence. Firstly, at independence where India's priorities changed from anti-colonial nationalist movement that had included all Indians around the world, to a nation state understanding which limited itself to internal integration. The Nehruvian encouragement of asking the Indian diaspora to integrate itself with the host country remained the dominant policy till the 1980s. The second policy shift happened when the ideological foreign policy of the Nehru years gave way to a more realistic regionally oriented policy of Indira Gandhi that could have improved government-NRI relations. But, the new approach appeared to be clear only in the second half of the 1980s under Rajiv Gandhi who handled the Fiji crisis. This was also the first time that the potential NRI was discussed and the banking system for the expatriates in the Gulf was facilitated. The third policy shift was evident in the liberalization period where despite the present suspicion among the Indian elites and government, they tried to encourage the NRIs to bring India out of its economic problems. [52] Therefore, whilst the ideals changed over time, the exclusion of the diaspora remained constant. The turn about has been visible with the BJP government coming to power. The mild alterations that were evident in the first forty years, the subsequent but slow changes have given way to an 'aggressive' policy towards the people of Indian origin.

These shifts in India's policy towards its diaspora could be identified with the pro-active foreign policy that it has been following for the last couple of years. The policy is pragmatic as it is trying to harness the Indian network that till now only exists through familial relations. Perhaps, it's the changed class composition along with the financial support of the NRIs that India at this moment considers to be beneficial for the country's development. The changed class composition can also be linked with the changed class structure of the ruling elite in India who wants now to be in true sense a *global citizen*. Therefore, the attempt is to be part of the political as well as economic decision-making at home.

The policy shift is perhaps clearly visible from the Nehruvian policy of calling upon the diaspora to integrate with the host societies, to the most recent development of offering dual citizenship to the NRIs. Nonetheless, the credit of the clear policy shift can be attributed to the Rao government of 1991 which broke the link with traditions set in 1947 by Nehru. The BJP government has only moved further in that direction. But, the controversial issue of dual citizenship will need to be resolved before the government can hope for any benefits either in political or in economic terms. At this moment, it remains ambiguous and raises a number of questions that will need to be addressed. The declarations by the government of awarding the NRIs, commemorating 9 January as the NRIs day are superficial and fringe benefits in real terms. Despite, the praises and excess importance extended to the NRIs their contributions in actual economic terms or in any form of material inputs have been very nominal.

Notes

1. A number of ideas and themes delineated have been discussed in the paper Aparajita Gangopadhyay (2005). *India's Policy towards its Diaspora: Continuity and Change*, India Quarterly (New Delhi), October – December, 61 (4): 93-122.

2. Indian labour emigration under the indenture system first started in 1834 to Mauritius, Uganda and Nigeria. Later the labourers emigrated to Guyana (1838), New Zealand (1840), Hong Kong (1841), Trinidad and Tobago (1845), Malay (1845), Martinique and Guadeloupe (1854). Grenada, St.Lucia and St. Vincent (1856), Natal (1860), St. Kitts (1861), Japan and Surinam (1872), Jamaica (1873), Fiji (1879), Burma (1885), Canada (1904) and Thailand (1910). Under the indenture system some 1.5 million persons migrated.

3. The Kangani (derived from Tamil kankani, meaning foreman or overseer) system prevailed in the recruitment of labour for emigration to Ceylon and Malaya. A variant of this system, called the maistry (derived from Tamil maistry, meaning supervisor) system was practised in the recruitment of labour for emigration to Burma. Under these systems the kangani or maistry (himself an Indian immigrant) recruited families of Tamil labourers from villages in the erstwhile Madras Presidency. Under these systems the labourers were legally free, as they were not bound by any contract or fixed period of service. These systems, which began in the first and third quarter of the nineteenth century, were abolished in 1938. Quoted from N. Jayaram. 2004. *The Indian Diaspora: Dynamics of Migration*. New Delhi, Thousand Oaks, London: Sage Publications, pp.17-20.

4. There was a steady trickle of emigration of members of trading communities from Gujarat and Punjab to South Africa and East Africa (Kenya, Tanzania and Uganda), and those from South India to South East Asia. Most labourers immigrated to East Africa to work on the railroad construction. These emigrants were not officially sponsored: they themselves paid their "passage" and they were "free" in the sense that they were not

bound by any contract.

5. Y. Ghai and D. Ghai, eds., (1970) Portrait of a Minority – Asians in East Africa, Nairobi, OUP, pp. 8-9.

6. Hugh Tinker, (1993) *A* New System of Slavery: The Export of Indian Labour Overseas, 1830-1920, London, Hansib Publishing Limited. quoted from Jayaram, op cit.

7. Though the colonial government enacted a few legislative directives for the protection and well being of the indentured labour in plantation barracks, they themselves violated these directives more often than not. Subsequently, on the request of the Colonial Government of India, the Secretary of State for Colonies had appointed a number of commissions of inquiry in order to seek justice against discrimination and exploitation of Indian labour. But, neither the commissions nor the reports contributed in any concrete manner in lessening their appalling conditions. Moreover, some such reports brought out the horrifying existing conditions, and thus were not made public for fear of shame; one such example is the report submitted by the West Indies Royal Commission in 1940. The only policy that the government followed was to export sufficient low paid work force to run the plantations. Other such instances of the British neglect of the Indian labour were evident also in the early part of the century. For example the Wragg Commission reported in 1887 that the Indian traders had the right to go to any part of the British Empire, since by trading in the remote parts they would provide the white population with useful services.

8. M.C. Lall (2001), India's Missed Opportunity—India's Relationship with Non-Resident Indians, Hampshire, Ashgate Publishing Ltd., pp. 27-28 and 84.

9. Ibid.

10. Ibid., p. 42.

11. Ibid., p. 43.

12. Ibid., pp. 91-92.

13. Ibid., p. 95.

14. Ibid., p. 76.

15. Bhiku Parekh, *The Indian Diaspora*, in Jagat K. Motwani, Mahin Gosine and Jyoti Barot-Motwani, eds., (1993) The Global Indian Diaspora: Yesterday, Today and Tomorrow ,Global Organization of People of Indian Origin, New York, pp. 8-9.

16. For instance, in 1947, hundreds of Indians in Jamaica organised

'back to India' demonstrations, but nothing came out of it. Similarly in 1948, several Trinidadian Indians threatened to commit mass suicide unless their government agreed to facilitate their return to India. In spite of Nehru's appeal they came but most of them returned back. Ibid., pp. 9-10.

17. Ministry of External Affairs Annual Report (MEA), New Delhi, 1991-92.

18. Lok Sabha Debates, 8 March 1948.

19. Sunil Khilnani, (1997), The Idea of India, London, Hamish Hamilton, p.167.

20. Anirudh Gupta quoted in P. Bhatia (1972),Indian Ordeal in Africa ,Teen Murti Library, New Delhi, pp. 121-122.

21. Parekh, op cit., p. 10.

22. Srikant Kumar Dutt (1981), India's Relations with Developing Countries: A Study of the Political economy of Indian Investment, Aid, Overseas Banking & Insurance, London School of Economics, London, pp. 93 (Ph.D. Thesis).

23. Lall, op cit., p. 99.

24. Tinker contends that despite India not approving of dual nationality, some East African Indians who were intensely proud of India's newly independent status obtained an Indian passport without surrendering existing citizenship rights. H. Tinker (1977), The Banyan Tree: Overseas Emigrants from India, Pakistan and Bangladesh, Oxford, Oxford University Press, quoted from Ibid., p. 100.

25. In fact, even the Department of Overseas Indians that had been set up in 1941 had been transformed to that of Commonwealth Relations in 1944. U. Mahajani, India and the People of Indian Origin Abroad, in M.S. Rajan, ed., (1976) India's Foreign Relations during the Nehru Era, Bombay , Asia Publishing House, p. 22, 290.

26. Parekh, op cit., p. 10.

27. Ibid.

28. Ibid.

29. Lall, op cit., pp. 2-4.

30. MEA Annual Report 1990-1991, p. 82.

31. Lok Sabha Debates (Parliament House, New Delhi), Q. 271, August 2, 1991.

32. Some such important incentives were: NRI investment in real estate development; 100 percent investment in 34 high priority

industries; Maximum limit of portfolio investment increased from 5 percent to 24 percent; Investment in India Development Bonds; Approval of investment and technical collaboration on automatic basis; Establishment of a Chief Commissioner for NRIs; Exemption of FERA to NRIs on various issues etc.

33. Lall, op cit., pp. 163-165.
34. N.H. Khan, Home Sweet Home, 26 April 1998 (internet) in Lall, op cit., p.168.
35. *Dual Citizenship for NRIs Likely Soon*, The Telegraph, 10 March 1992, and *Rao Opposes Dual Citizenship for NRIs*, Statesman, 18 May1994.
36. Lall, op cit., p. 168.
37. Ibid., p. 4.
38. Parekh, op cit., p. 10.
39. Mahin Gosine, *The Forgotten Children of India: A Global Perspective*, in Jagat K. Motwani, Mahin Gosine and Jyoti Barot-Motwani, eds., (1993) The Global Indian Diaspora: Yesterday, Today and Tomorrow ,Global Organization of People of Indian Origin, New York, p.19.
40. Davesh Kapur, Indian *Diaspora as a Strategic Asset*, EPW, 1 February 2003, pp. 445-448.
41. Almost all remaining restrictions on trade and other economic sectors were removed, and India became part of the World Trading Organisation (WTO).
42. The main clauses of the PIO card are: (a) No registration with the FRRO (Foreign Regional Registration Office) if the stay does not exceed 180 days. (b) For acquisition, holding, transfer and disposal of immovable properties PIO cardholders would be given parity with the NRI nationals. (c) Children of the PIO cardholders will be treated at par with the children of NRI nationals with respect to admission to education institutions in India. (d) They would be eligible for NRI nationals housing schemes. Lall, n.7, p. 197.
43. *Chennai Declaration*, BJP News Report, 28-29 December 1999.
44. The committee included Sri R L Bhatia, Congress MP and former Minister of State for External Affairs, J R Hiremath, former Diplomat and Baleshwar Agrawal, Secretary-General of the Antar Rashtriya Sahyog Parishad. An additional secretary in the Ministry of External Affairs was the member-secretary. The terms of reference of the Committee were: (1) To review the

status of PIOs and NRIs in the context of the Constitutional Provisions. (2) Laws and rules applicable to them, both in India and the countries of their residence. (3) Study the characteristics, aspirations, attitudes, requirements, strengths and weaknesses of the Indian diaspora and its expectations from India. (4) Study the role PIOs and NRIs may play in the economic, social and technological development of India. (5) Examine the current regime governing the travel and stay of PIOs and investments by PIOs in India. The committee will recommend measures to resolve the problems faced by NRIs, and evolve a broad but flexible policy framework and country-specific plans for forging a mutually beneficial relationship and for facilitating their interaction and participation in India's economic development.

45. Part I contains the Letter of Transmission of the Report to Government by the committee Chairman; the Orders of the Ministry of External Affairs setting up the Committee describing its terms of reference; the Foreword; the Executive Summary and the Acknowledgements. Part II is a detailed examination of the genesis and particular circumstances of the Indian Diaspora in selected countries and regions. This section concludes with a global perspective of other Diasporas and the nature and extent of their interaction with their countries of origin. Part III contained the three Interim Reports that were submitted by the Committee to Government some months ago and which have been graciously accepted by our Prime Minister today. These are: the fee reduction in the PIO Card Scheme, celebration of Pravasi Bharatiya Divas on January 9 each year and the institution of 10 Pravasi Bharatiya Samman Awards. Part IV of the Report includes detailed examination and recommendations on major Diaspora issues in the fields of Consular and related matters, Culture, Economic Development, Investment, International Trade, Industry, Tourism, Education, Health, Media, Science & Technology and Philanthropy. This part of the Report also deals with dual citizenship and the creation of a single window dedicated organisation to interact with the Diaspora. Part V of the Report contains the detailed Conclusions and Recommendations of the Committee on the entire gamut of the expectations, needs and requirements of our agenda for the Indian Diaspora. See
http://meadev.nic.in/news/offical/20020108/official1.htm

46. Hindu (Bangalore), 9 January 2002.
47. Under the 1955 Indian Citizenship Act, anyone who had 'voluntarily acquired the citizenship of another country...(to) cease to be a citizen of India'.
48. Jayati Ghosh, *More Equal than Others*, Frontline (Chennai), vol.19, no.2, 19 January-1 February 2002.
49. Ibid.
50. *Government Keen on Forging Ties with NRIs*, The Hindu /Hindustan Times (New Delhi), 6 October 2001.
51. See Manmohan Hands Over OCI Cards *http://www.thehindu.com/2006/01/08/stories/200601080400100 0.htm* and Manmohan Singh Tells Diaspora to Help Build A New India *http://www.thehindu.com/2007/01/08/stories/200701080971010 0.htm*
52. See, n. 46, pp. 4-5.

References

Cohen Robin, (1999) Global Diaspora: An Introduction, London, UCL Press.

Gangopadhyay Aparajita (2005), *India's Policy towards its Diaspora: Continuity and Change*, India Quarterly (New Delhi), October – December, 61 (4), pp. 93-122.

Ghai, Y. and D. Ghai eds., (1970) Portrait of a Minority – Asians in East Africa, Nairobi, OUP.

Ghosh, Jayati (2002), *More Equal than Others*, Frontline (Chennai), 19 (2).

Jayaram, N. *Introduction: The Study of Indian Diaspora*, N. Jayaram, ed., (2004) The Indian Diaspora: Dynamics of Migration , New Delhi, Sage Publications, pp. 15-43.

Kapur, Davesh (2003), *Indian Diaspora as a Strategic Asset*, EPW, 38 (5): 445-448.

Lall, M.C, (2001) India's Missed Opportunity: India's Relationship with the Non Resident Indians, Ashgate, Burlington, Singapore and Sydney.

Motwani, Jagat K., Mahin Gosine and Jyoti Motwani ed., (1993) Global Indian Diaspora: Yesterday, Today and Tomorrow, New York, GOPIO Publication.

Narayanan R. and Ashok Shrivastava. *Diasporic Hindus of the Caribbean with Special Reference to Trinidad*, in T.S. Rukmani, ed., (2001) Hindu Diaspora: Global Perspectives, New Delhi, Munshiram Manoharlal Publishers, pp. 165 – 190.

Rajan M.S.ed. (1976),India's Foreign Relations during the Nehru Era, Bombay, Asia Publishing House.

Tinker H (1977), The Banyan Tree: Overseas Emigrants from India, Pakistan and Bangladesh. Oxford, Oxford University Press.

3

Nehruvian Legacy: Democratic Socialism and Strategy of Economic Development: An Appraisal

P. Arjun Rao

Jawaharlal Nehru's love for the country and countrymen did not have any boundary for demarcation. His commitment to the economic development of the country was beyond question. He was impressed with the rapid development of Soviet Union in a short period through planning. He admired the individual freedom found in the West and considered it equally important for the growth and development of the society. Thus, he adopted socialism and democracy that are diametrically opposite for India's development – by integrating the good virtues of both the systems, and these formed the cornerstone of India's governance and development. The cardinal principles of economic development of the country were to achieve self-sufficiency and to raise the standard of living of its people apart from laying strong foundation for future development. Nehru's vision of development was reflected in the Mahalanobis model of development that gave first priority of investment in heavy industries, which were mostly to in the public sector.

The relevance of the policies and the strategies for economic development pursued by Nehru within the sphere of democratic socialism might appear to be redundant under the present circumstances. While discussing these two aspects, one should not forget the conditions prevalent when the said policies were laid down. Those were the times when Soviet Union's achievements were most impressive and appealing to Third World countries. Even the West started thinking afresh on the premise of planning; to a certain extent, planning as a strategy was accepted in certain sectors of their economy. One has to understand that in India a large number, say to the extent of 60 percent of enterprises, are into private sector by way of retailing. In a way, the economy as regards investments by government, to a large extent, are in public sector; however private sector also existed and operated in the non-core and non-strategic sectors from the point of view of security and general welfare.

Even in the Liberalization, Privatisation and Globalisation (LPG) scenario, the Indian Government is the largest investor in the public sector under any standards. The PSUs are competing and making huge profits. There was nothing wrong in the policies pursued by Nehru but people mattered who were responsible to implement such policies. We enjoy a socialistic pattern of economy **without violence??** And we enjoy individual freedom and dignity—the cardinal elements of democracy—peacefully with greater emphasis on social justice. The experience of privatisation around the globe is staggering. There is a great divide and gap between the rich and the poor on account of pursuing LPG. In a country like India, where mass poverty, illiteracy, unemployment, and under employment are rampant, LPG policies might aggravate the situation and lead to violent protests. The state in under developing and developing countries cannot absolve its responsibility towards poor and downtrodden. The State has every obligation to protect the country's poor against the exploitative tendencies found under LPG scenario. The point of intolerance found among the countries against LPG might compel the governments all over the globe to revert their policies and, perhaps, a day would certainly come when policies pursued by Nehru, i.e. policies of democratic socialism would be more acceptable and help in the real all round development of society. The research paper deals in brief critically the idea of democratic socialism and strategy for economic development and enlightens about LPG and its implications finally leading to reversal of policies.

Indian Economic Scenario in 1950s

The Indian economic scenario, immediately after independence, was very depressing and miserable; some of the glaring problems plaguing the country and its populace are as follows:

- Majority of the Indian population was entrenched in mass poverty.
- Illiteracy and untrained labour.
- Feudal domination in the agriculture sector.
- Rain-dependant agriculture system.
- Poor transportation infrastructure.
- Poor communication system.
- Unemployment and under employment.
- Very poor energy production.
- Inadequate banking system.
- Women participation was negligible in any sector of the economy and governance as well.

Development through Planning

India, under the able leadership of Jawahar Lal Nehru, had to steer the state from such a miserable economy onto the path of development. India opted a course of development through planning, though the West felt that planning was regimentation. Capitalism guided Western nations' economy. Western democracies professed belief in capitalism; and market economy was considered the cornerstone for every kind of economic activity. Socialism was unacceptable to major democracies. But India, under the leadership of Nehru, adopted a middle path for her development accepting mixed economy wherein public and private enterprises co-exist. The magnitude of problems invited India to undertake a huge national economic effort possible only through the State intervention. Therefore, in the context explained supra, India adopted planning as a lever of social and economic change.

Nehru visited European countries and also Russia during the freedom struggle. He was deeply impressed with Russia's rapid development and achievements within a short time. In fact, Russia's efforts towards development commenced only from 1928. In a way, Nehru borrowed the idea of socialism from Russians.

However, one should remember that Nehru was a great admirer of democratic values of capitalist society. Nehru was also tremendously influenced by Western education and economic philosophy; he strongly believed that democratic values were more pertinent and important for the all round development of society. Thus, Nehru adopted to follow the virtues of two extreme and divergent systems and he termed the course he chose as *democratic socialism*. It is in the interest of good academics to understand briefly the theoretical framework of two divergent systems to know and comprehend precisely the democratic socialism as a concept. In a way, democratic socialism could be described as the blend of two systems – capitalism and socialism.

Democratic Socialism

Karl Marx and Frederick Engels provided theoretical foundations as basis of socialism. The chief plank for such a theory was to abolish private ownership of the means of production. Secondly, they were of the opinion that the private property was the primary cause of socio-economic ills. The process of such a theory culminated into planning with complete nationalisation; and such a policy was to achieve the growth that would eradicate poverty, and remove unemployment. According to socialist theory, economic development through planning could solve all the above stated problems. The targets of economic planning in Russia were achieved and the country made rapid strides in the area of development. Russia's rapid industrialisation inspired several newly independent under-developed countries and earned a lot of admiration. Even the West started feeling the impact of such a rapid development with higher growth rate that Russia achieved. But in the process Russian citizens lost their individual freedom and also it cost the lives of several millions who were considered enemies of socialism.

Great Depression and State Intervention

While this was the case of Russia, it becomes inevitable to think about the developments that took place in capitalist democracies during the period under discussion. The Great Depression of 1929-33 shook the very foundations of people's faith in the price-mechanism as an instrument of self-adjusting mechanism. Though the state intervention into economy was abolished, United States had to step into the shoes of the mechanism of state intervention to play a positive role into the socio-economic lives of its citizens. The Depression made the capitalist societies and governments to depart from the earlier stand they pursued on economic policies; and it was realised that the governments could play an effective role by making efforts to eventually reduce poverty, misery, unemployment, under-employment, illiteracy, ignorance etc. Lord Keynes' advice and his public works programs influenced capitalist nations to take far-reaching decisions and to adopt a policy of State intervention to play a positive role in the domain of State economy. Earlier, West considered State intervention as an unholy affair. At the same time, it should also be borne in mind, which capitalist democracies did not rule out the faith in private property and individual freedom. It may not be out of place to state here, that the author remembers reading a statement in *The Hindu* some years back, which read as follows:

Freedom or Food

Eisenhower met Stalin at some place. After pleasantries the discussion went around which system of government was good—whether democracy, which gave right to property and individual liberty or socialism, which was authoritarian and unfavourable to individual freedom. Stalin became stoic and gave an anecdote to the query which ran as follows:

"A citizen was imprisoned for a few days without food. He was quite hungry and looking weak and pale. The sentry desired to know from him whether the wanted food or individual freedom." Food" was the reply from the imprisoned.

Stalin laughed heartily and Eisenhower looked stunned. Though individual freedom is a *must* but at the same no citizen can remain without food. The individual freedom comes later in preference to food."

Nehru and Democratic Socialism

While there are a few aspects of capitalism and socialism as merits and demerits, Nehru chose the path of a synthesis arising out of both the system. The thinking of Nehru on democratic socialism is explained hereunder:

Democracy and socialism are means for establishing a society where all the citizens enjoy equal opportunities to education, employment, healthcare and where there is no exploitation. The ultimate goal of democratic socialism is free and all round development of its citizenry. Socialism takes care of all the said aspects. Democracy ensures the freedom of the citizens and all round growth of human personality.

Lord Keynes observed in 1926, "The world is not so governed from above that, private and social interests always coincide. It is not a correct deduction from the principles of economics that enlightened self-interest always operates in the public interest.

Nor is it true that self-interest is generally enlightened." [1] That way Keynes proved right when the Great Depression exhibited hollowness of the classical thinkers' claim of the smooth working of the economic system. Though he admired some of the merits of capitalism like competition and efficiency in production, he was critical of socialism that would not allow individual freedom in the sphere of economy and politics. But he was also of the opinion that control and direction were necessary in the modern society. According to Pigou, the system of Socialist Central Planning, if it could be effectively organised, would be in many respects preferable to our existing capitalist system." [2]

Since both the systems had some merits, a compromise between high degree of state intervention in the sphere economy and free capitalist economy could be the basis for democratic socialism. As stated earlier, Nehru came under the influence of both the systems. He desired that the virtues found in democracy and socialism could form the basis for the concept of democratic socialism whereby both the public and private sectors could co-exist and flourish. It may not be out of place, here, to state that India, soon after attaining independence, did not have the capability to make heavy investments in various sectors on a large scale for the development through the Five-Year Plans. Nehru's Government allowed the private sector to operate in the sphere of country's economy though prime importance and share was given to the public sector. Jawahar Lal Nehru, the architect of Indian Planning, strongly believed that socialism and democracy were the means for establishing a society in India whereby all the citizens could enjoy equal opportunities to employment, health care, education, etc. He also had faith that democratic socialism could abolish exploitation of one class by another. In other words, for Nehru, democratic socialism was a vision of new and modern India.

Public Sector Undertakings in India

The Public Sector share in the investment for development was huge since it was contemplated that it would generate and augment finances in addition to equi-distribution and social development. Investment made in the public enterprises took the economy to commanding heights. However, as time passed, it was soon realised that the nation cannot afford to continue to subsidize the losses incurred by public enterprises. In addition, the country's economy was in precarious condition, which ultimately led to the mortgage of its gold reserves with Bank of England to tide over the foreign exchange crises. The impact of LPG–Liberalisation, Privatisation and Globalisation (LPG) is making inroads into even a land-locked country like Bhutan, and India could not afford to be an exception to such a phenomenon.

The performance of public enterprises has been quite unsatisfactory for the following reasons:

- Political interference in day to day administration.
- Political influence in the decision-making process of the PSUs treating it as, almost, a government department.
- Adoption of bureaucratic practices in corporate undertakings headed by civil servants.
- Over capitalisation.
- Mounting losses.
- Labour indiscipline.
- Irrational price policy.
- Employing more manpower than actually required.
- Delay in grounding the projects resulting in rise in construction costs etc.
- Managerial inefficiency etc.

The above stated factors are man-made. There is nothing wrong with the concept and philosophy of public enterprises. The wind, since the collapse of Soviet Union and the changing economic scenario since 1991, is blowing towards liberalisation, privatisation and globalisation (LPG). The Nehruvian model of development i.e. heavy investment in public sector is slowly giving in to new economic changes. Hence it is the system failure but not the failure of the concept and philosophy of public enterprises. One should note here, that under the present competitive economic environment, public enterprise performance is encouraging and PSUs are being proved as assets to national exchequer. The Government of India and state governments in Indian Union should not go in for privatising the profit making PSUs for the sake of privatisation. The nation has to gear up all its energies to further industrialise and produce rather than sell the existing industries to earn which is a faulty economic policy.

Nehru's Model for Economic Development

Indian history of economic development owes much to Jawaharlal Nehru. He was emotionally committed to the development of India through planning. He was of the firm opinion that India should develop through industrialisation. According to him "If we are to industrialise, it is primary importance that we must have the heavy industries which would build industries." [3] Nehru was associated with the subject of economic development of India even during the period of freedom movement. He used to elaborate on the steps that would independent India would take for its economic development. He could visualise a developed and modern India. As stated earlier, and at the risk of repetition, India opt development through planning after attaining independence. The planners devised Five-Year Plans for development.

The First Five Year Plan did not have any strategy except giving importance to agriculture, irrigation and power, which were basic requirements for industrialisation. During the process of formulation of Second Five Year Plan, it was realised that a long run development strategy was required. Nehru adopted Mahalanobis model, which focussed on rapid industrialisation with emphasis on heavy industries producing basic machines and basic metals. It was a heavy investment strategy for a strong and self-reliant economy and for avoiding dependence on imports of essential machinery and equipment. The same strategy continued for the Third Five Year Plan. It could raise the savings and investments rates in the country for remarkable development of infrastructure in the sectors of irrigation, energy, transport, communication etc. The dominant role, in almost all the sectors, was given to public sector. An appraisal of Mahalanobis model came in for criticism for the following shortcomings of the heavy industrialisation strategy.

Appraisal of the Development Model

It was argued that agriculture sector was neglected. But it should be noted here that Nehru understood that India was basically an agriculture country and it was the basic occupation of 75 percent to 80 percent of the population. He could have not missed this factor. To quote Nehru in this regard, "We shall find that this industrial progress cannot be achieved without agricultural advance and progress. The fact is that the two cannot be separated. They are intimately connected because agricultural progress is not possible without industry, without tools, without new method and techniques." [4] But in practice one could see that there was a great disparity in allocation from GDP i.e. 20 percent was against agriculture and 18-24 percent towards industries. Charm Singh, a severe critic of Nehru's concept of industrialisation and investment strategy opined, "Neglect of agriculture is, so to say, the original sin of the planners of India's destiny." [5]

Nehru-Mahalanobis model did not absolve itself from helping agricultural sector. According in this model, creation and investment in the infrastructure like power, transport and industries would certainly help agricultural sector's development by providing electricity, implements, fertilisers etc. to the agri-sector.

While Nehru-Mahalanobis model gave priority to heavy investment into heavy industries, it was not averse to the small scale and cottage industries or the agriculture sectors but the model opined that they could produce consumer goods. The model under discussion was well aware that investment into this sector was small compared to heavy industry and the further in-put, out-put ratio was also small. The gestation period was also short. According to Nehru, the test of a country's advance in industrialisation is heavy industry and not the small-scale industry, though he did not mean that small industries should be ignored. They are highly important in themselves for production and for employment. [6]

An Appraisal

The entire exercise in this paper centres on the concepts of democratic socialism and strategy for economic development pursued by Jawaharlal Nehru. The discussion points out that the policies adopted at that point of time were considered appropriate and suitable while laying down strong foundation for future sustainable growth and development. India could build the strong infrastructure for development by implementing Nehru-Mahalanobis model of economic development. It will become improper to state that such policies could not have been adopted and that there were several mistakes committed. It may not be safe and sound to say that all public policies are flowers. Even so called rational decisions made by the governments, thought to be appropriate at that point of time might be considered as irrational at a later stage or situation. It is all, relative in nature as well. Opposition parties opposing certain policies of erstwhile government, when they come to power toe the same line, which they opposed. It is easier to talk but it is always difficult to do. Every government should learn from its past mistakes and take correctional measures. The whole discussion made under appraisal is an endeavour to convey that all the policies pursued by Nehru might not be appropriate but could not be brushed aside as useless; also the fact remains that it was Nehru who laid a strong economic and democratic foundations. Most underdeveloped and developing countries still look to Nehru's economic plans to achieve self-sufficiency and to pursue independent policies.

Notes

1. J.M. Keynes, The End of Laissez Faire.
2. A.C. Pigou, (1937) Socialism vs. Capitalism.
3. Nehru's speech in the Parliament on the Draft Outline of the Third Plan 22.08.1960.
4. Government of India, Problems in Third Plan – The Framework, p. 35.
5. Charam Single, India's Economic Policy (Vikas), p. 90.

6. Government of India, Problem in the Third Plan, A Critical Review, p. 51.

4

Jawaharlal Nehru and the Congress Party of India

G. Gopa Kumar

The Indian National Congress has become one of the most successful mass organisations that fought against imperialism in the colonial history of the Afro-Asian and Latin American societies. Like the Institutional Revolutionary Party of Mexico which transformed itself from the role of a freedom movement to a ruling party and governed the state for over six decades, the Congress Party of India too transformed itself from the role of national movement to the task of a dominant party, especially during the first three decades of post-independent India. The Party is still the strongest national party, despites its setbacks since 1977, it was voted back to power in 1980, 1984, 1991, 2004 and 2009 elections. Since 2004 it has virtually accepted the reality of coalition politics at the national level, and in many states, the Congress had already become a senior partner in coalition governments. The focus of the paper here is to evaluate the synergy between the Congress Party and the Nehruvian contributions and review how far this linkage had influenced the nation building process in the decades that followed.

Launched on December 28, 1885 at the initiative of a British Officer Allan Octavian Hume, the initial idea of this interest group was to persuade British government to provide sufficient representation for educated Indians in the civil service. Many other socio-cultural and political movements of the period influenced the early destiny of the Congress like the Home Rule League, the Arya Samaj, the Brahma Samaj, the Swarajya Party, besides the social reformers like Raja Ram

Mohan Roy, Dayanantha Saraswathi, Swamy Vivekananda etc. The Congress reformed itself consequently from the ritual position of submitting representations to Her Majesty's government to that of an organisation with an ideological focus. This also led to the conflict in the organisation between moderates led by Gopalakrishana Gokhale and extremists led by Bal Gangadhara Tilak. The ideological division with in the Congress started in Surat in 1907 and the tempo continued up to 1916. By the time Mohandas Karam Chand Gandhi returned from South Africa and joined the Congress, the Swarajya leaders like Mothilal Nehru, C.R Das and others had started struggles focusing on the Legislature, using institutional process.

Jawaharlal Nehru was attracted towards the Congress movement even while he was continuing his education in Britain. He was sympathetic to the British Labour Party which later influenced his ideological perspective towards democratic socialism. On his return from England, he took up the mantle of a Barrister in United Province but soon gave up joining the Congress. Nehru's connections with Congress thus began in 1912. He attended the Bankipare (Patna) Congress presided over by Gokhale. [1] His first elected post was that of the Chairman of Allahabad Municipality. He worked closely with Congress led trade union, All India Trade Union Congress. He was elected the General Secretary of the AITUC in 1925. He had already established good rapport with Gandhiji. Along with other leaders like Govind Vallabh Pant, C. Rajagopalachari, Maulana Abdul Kalam Azad, Dr. Rajendra Prasad, Sardar Vallabhai Patel, Acharya Kripalani, Nehru and Gandhi were able to transform the Congress soon into a mass movement.

On the whole, Nehru was President of the Indian National Congress six times and before that he served as General Secretary of the AICC from 1923 to 1925 (Table 4.1). He was also the President of the All India Trade Union Congress for the meeting held at Nagpur in 1929. His role and contribution in the AICC meetings influenced the collective thinking of the organization considerably. For instance, the declaration of the *Purna Swaraj* in the Lahore Session of 1929, the drafting of Fundamental Rights, the ideas and perspectives of National Planning in the Karachi session of 1931 and the contributions of Foreign Relations Committee of AICC became landmarks in the history of modern India.

Table 4.1: Nehru as President of Indian National Congress

S. No.	Year	Session
1.	1929-1930	Lahore
2.	1936	Lucknow
3.	1937	Faizpur
4.	1951-1952	New Delhi
5.	1953	Hyderabad
6.	1954	Calcutta

Source:http//en.wikepedia.org/indiannationalcongress#jawaharlalnehru.

Understanding the Nehruvian perspectives in the larger framework of modern India has always been a challenging task. Many scholars had attempted and this process will continue in future as well. His roles were numerous—the architect of modern India, the crucial link between Gandhiji and traditional Indian society, one of the top leaders of Congress party in the Gandhian era and the crucial leader in post-independence period. He was a visionary but a realist as well and was sensitive to the ground realities of the sub-continent.

When the Nehru and Congress were criticized for being responsible for the partition of the country Nehru sharply reacted—"Partition was not only the responsibility of the Congress but also other parties, including Akali Dal and Maha Sabha. The consent of these organisations, now vociferous in their accusation against the Congress, had also been obtained to the Partition Plan in an attempt to clear the body politic of the communal virus. It was a painful operation on the body of

India but the Congress tolerated it in the hope that communalism would be banished from the land. The communalism of the Muslim League pattern went away to Pakistan, but unfortunately a new type of communalism had reared its ugly head in India. [2] Interestingly, Nehru and the Congress, though not against the creation of linguistic provinces, opposed it whenever it was wedded to communalism. But the post-Nehruvian era produced a different picture as could be evinced in the territorial disputes between Punjab and Haryana, after the creation of three separate states (Punjab, Haryana and Himachal Pradesh), during the era of Mrs. Indira Gandhi. On the question of Uniform Civil Code, Nehru reluctantly permitted each religious community to retain its civil laws or *personal courts*. [3] Later, this provision embodied in Article 44 of the Indian Constitution became a major controversy both on religious and gender issues and it still remains an unsettled one.

Although Nehru was exposed to the ideology of socialism in Europe, he was aware of the suitability and application to the specific context of India. Therefore, despite his strong attraction to the ideology of socialism, he warned the Congress Socialist Party, in the 1930s, not to neglect their perspective on what would work in the Indian condition. [4] Similarly, when Nehru was anxious to define the content of freedom in economic terms, Gandhiji was alarmed and partly succeeded in persuading Nehru to tone down the divisive aspects of such a definition. [5] Again, Nehru was aware of the fact that democracy has developed along with capitalism in the West. This was not the kind of development needed for India. Therefore, he wanted to use the democratic process in India to set in motion the development of a greater measure of social justice for the masses in some form of socialism. Nehru believed that democratic processes in different societies acquired different goals and in India, with the vast extremes of riches and poverty, it would have its drift towards a greater measure of social equality. [6]

The critiques who were attacking Nehru for not sharpening his theoretical framework on socialism perhaps realized later, how practical and visionary he was in shaping the Indian concept of socialism. As Chairman of the National Planning Commission appointed by the Indian National Congress in 1938, Nehru had laid down the general principles which would govern land policy in India after British had withdrawn. In its Nagpur session of 1959 the Congress under the leadership of Nehru adopted a resolution seeking a programme of cooperative farming in India. [7] Nehru appealed to raise the living standards of the people and remove all the obstacles that come in the way of the economic growth of the nation – "if we want to make economic progress, it means producing more wealth...what is produced by everyone working together constitute the wealth of the country. [8] Nehru's concept of socialism in India is very clear in these statements.

Many foreign observers had noticed that there was much in common between Gandhi, Patel and Rajendra Prasad on domestic and external policies while Nehru's was of a distinct position. But to the common people, Nehru's denunciation of affluence did not seem to conflict with Gandhi's ideas and his belief in *Sarvodaya*. [9] To be sure, Nehru and Gandhi linkages had shaped into a new bond of democratic and national sentiments, unheard in the history of India's leadership. Edward Luce states that "to many in the villages and fields of India, it provides a political narrative that links their feudal past to a democratic present and hopefully to a more prosperous future". [10]

Inside Democracy in Congress: Initial Experiences
Congress has always been a store house of multiple interest groups which in turn articulated their demands into the shaping of policies of the party. Since its inception, it carried on the strength and consequently accommodated extreme diverse groups—ideological, social, cultural, economic, etc. The competition and conflict that underwent inside the

Congress shaped a unique style of inner party democracy. For this instance, the movement character of the Congress which began with the Gandhian era was preceded by ideological competition between moderates and extremists. Prior to that, the Indian National Congress had limited goals and concerns as formulated by A.O. Hume, W.C. Banerjee and others. It was ritually sending representation to Her Majesty's Government and the major demand of the Congress during the period was that the government may provide opportunity for educated Indians in the colonial bureaucracy.

The Gandhian era (1920-1948) witnessed the rapid growth of the organization taking up the challenge against colonial power as evinced through various movements, struggles and agitations. It was this phase of the evolution that made the Congress a major mass movement unheard in the history of anti-colonial struggle anywhere in the world. The presence of selfless leaders beside Gandhi and Nehru, Maulana Abdul Kalam Azad, Motilal Nehru, Sardar Vallabhai Patel, Acharya Kripalani, C. Rajagopala Achari, Purushothama Das Tandon, Dr. Rajendra Prasad, G.V. Pant, Lal Bahadur Shastri, Morarji Desai, U.N. Dhebar and many others provided an excellent opportunity for the movement to accelerate its non-violent, anti-colonial struggle. The country was so fortunate that many of these leaders continue to guide the Congress even after independence and in the process, strengthened the institution of the state and its structures.

Although, Gandhiji argued for the dissolution of the Congress soon after independence and instead transform it into a voluntary body called Lok Sevak Sangh, Nehru insisted that the Congress must continue to serve the nation and build the modern India. Gandhi's fear was that the movement's graduation to power would reduce it to a power-seeking machine by taking the credit for achieving the freedom for the country. Although, many of the concerns raised by Gandhi were proved true, Nehru had an equally strong point in his argument. Since, no other party had developed to accept the responsibility on their shoulders of guiding the country; Nehru found the efficacy and utility of retaining the Congress in the post-independence phase as well. Despite the issues of one *party dominance*, India was able to improve upon parliamentary democracy, thanks to the public support to the Congress party at least for the first three decades. By this time, party building in the nation had improved upon considerably leading to the shaping of a multi-party system with different wave lengths at the regional level.

Differences persisted in the Congress movement throughout the period of freedom struggle but this enabled a transformation process inside the Congress which by this time became the sole unifying force of the country .The first public clash between Nehru and Gandhi occurred in December 1927 at the Madras session of the AICC on the question of Congress's political goal. Gandhi stood for dominion status while Nehru for complete independence. The struggle was resolved in 1929 only at the Lahore session with the adoption of complete independence. [11] The Congress Working Committee had acted primarily as the chief policymaker for the movement and the Chief Executive of the organisation. [12] Nehru's attempt in 1936 to rehabilitate the mass base of the organization with associating trade unions and peasant bodies was thwarted by the senior leaders who feared that it would strengthen the left wing in the Congress. They suggested for establishing mass contact committee as a means for expanding membership within the existing party framework. [13] This step in many ways was helpful to the Congress since it was actively involved in other social struggles like removing untouchability, anti-liquor struggle, temple entry movements, etc.

Similarly, on the issue of continuing freedom struggle in the princely states, divergent opinions prevailed in the congress. It was Gandhiji's idea that since the struggle had to be focused against the Britishers, the Congress should not over-energize freedom struggle in the princely states. But, the

Congress Working Committee had to yield to the pressures of regional leaders and agreed to set up provincial pro-Congress bodies, yet independent of the Congress, so that the tempo of freedom struggle in these areas would not be halted. But later developments proved that this policy also led to the rise of regionalism which negatively affected the trajectory of the Congress Party in the post-1947 periods.

James Manor notes that Nehru did not establish his ascendancy within the Congress Party *High Command* until 1951. [14] With the passing away of Sardar Patel in December 1950, there was no leader that could command similar appeal and influence like that of Nehru. But this does not mean that he had converted the party colleagues as his subordinates. For instance, Nehru did not dabble in routine state politics although it was rare for a Chief Minister to retain his office unless Nehru reposed some measure of confidence in him. As a matter of fact, the *Nehruvian consensus* was invariably synchronizing with the *Congress concerns*. [15] However, the dismissal of first elected Communist government in India (E.M.S. Namboodiripad Government in Kerala) on July 31, 1959 raised a huge controversy.

Although, many would argue that Nehru was responsible for invoking Article 356 against the duly elected non-Congress government, following the *liberation struggle* (1958-1959), the crucial role played by KPCC cannot be slighted in this case. Once the powerful communal pressure groups created the band wagon of an anti-communist struggle, the KPCC utilized the opportunity and pressurized the High Command. Thus, it is clear that, unlike today, Pradesh Congress Committees and the regional leaders had enjoyed prominence in decision making levels of CWC. There are other evidences to support this argument. The decision of senior leaders to nominate Dr. Rajendra Prasad as the party's candidate for Union Presidency for a second term in 1956 was certainly not of Nehru's choice. Robin Jeffrey points out as follows—"a frequent criticism of Congress Party was that it's Chief Ministers in some states were 'getting too much of their own way' because Nehru was 'uncomfortably aware' of their value to the party in the state". [16]

This was proved true again once we consider the emergence of *Congress Syndicate* with regional leaders like K. Kamaraj, Athulya Ghosh, S. Nijalingappa, G.B. Pant, etc. emerging as kingmakers of CWC. Their strength improved considerably in the later years when Nehru's health started declining. These state leaders resolved significant issues in advance and played the role of a coterie inside the CWC. Even though, the *Kamaraj Plan* was designed both by Nehru and Kamaraj, at one point Nehru was willing to step down from the post of Prime Minister and serve the party organization. But the party was equally important for Nehru, argues Robin Jeffrey, "for Nehru, as Prime Minister, the advantages of such a party lay first, in the apparent fulfilment of promises about having the 'people,' participate in the government of free India; secondly, in the capacity to organize election campaigns; and thirdly, in the potential for explaining and implementing government programmes". [17]

In turn, for the Congress, Nehru was the epicentre of political leadership—as the unchallenged leader of Congress Parliamentary · Party and the Council of Ministers, the President of the Party during 1951-54 period, architect of India's foreign policy and economic planning besides the pride of place he enjoyed at the international level. The tussle between Purushothama Das Tandon, the party President and Prime Minister Nehru ended up in the dominance of Nehru compelling the frustrated Tandon to comment that "the Congress Party has become the slave of the government". Nehru's response was different "I agree entirely with those friends and comrades of ours who have objected to the high offices of Prime Minister and Congress President being held by one and the same person. However I am here at your bidding and yet I feel a little unhappy that I should have been chosen once again as Congress President I tried hard that this should not occur and pleaded with my comrades in the Congress to make some other choice. [18]

Until 1969, the internal party elections to various offices were held constitutionally and regularly. The Plenary session elected from various part of the country brought 3000 delegates and followed up by the election of AICC, Party President and similar offices at the highest level. When Mrs. Indira Gandhi was brought as the interim President of the Congress in 1959, Nehru was personally unhappy. He said, "normally speaking, it is not a good thing for my daughter to come as Congress president when I am the Prime Minister. [19]

Undoubtedly, the passing of the objective of the socialistic pattern of society by the party was at the initiative and imagination of Nehru. Once the objective was endorsed by the National Development Council the Cabinet, the Congress Parliamentary Party and Lok Sabha, it was ratified by the Congress Working Committee. Subsequently, the AICC held in Avadi, Madras, in January 1955 passed a resolution which stated that "in order to realize the object of Congress Constitution and further the objectives stated in the Preamble and Directive Principles of State Policy in the Constitution of India, planning should take place with a view to the establishment of a socialistic pattern of society, where the principal means of production are under social ownership or control, production is progressively speeded up and there is equitable distribution of national wealth". [20]

Nehru's differences with Sardar Patel were extreme on many grounds. Even there was a strong belief among scholars that had not Patel passed away on December 16, 1950; the situation would have led to the rise of a strong rival organisation to the Congress Party, led by Sardar Patel. Indeed, their differences were not strictly personal but on ideological and policy grounds. They differed on the approach towards communalism, communists at the global and regional levels, economic policies including agrarian reforms, etc.

Pandit Nehru was almost on the verge of leaving the Congress Party because he was finding it difficult to get reconcile to Sardar Patel's resolve to fight communist aggression, outside and inside to the last ditch. [21] Similarly, the party's approach towards Hindu Mahasabha and RSS raised issues in the organisation. Nehru had challenged the Hindu traditionalists within the Congress to accept his doctrine of secularism or to incur the charge of communalism. [22]

Since India had undergone a tremendous phase of communal conflict, Nehru was sensitive to the whole issue – although, with the partition, one form of communalism disappeared, other forms of communalism both from the Hindu Right and the minorities were on the making in the body politic. Not surprisingly, in one of his first international media briefings, responding to a question from the correspondent of the Washington Post, Nehru remarked that "the greatest challenge before me as the Prime Minister of India is how to transform a deeply traditional society into a modern one." Shashi Tharoor notes that Nehru foresaw the danger of majority communalism and its indirect linkages with nationalism—"since, most of us are Hindus, the distinction between Hindu nationalism and Indian nationalism could be all two easily blurred. [23]

On the question of All India Muslim League, Nehru firmly believed that the very birth of the organisation in 1906 was meant to keep the Muslims away from the Congress. In his view, Muhammed Ali Jinnah's policies basically were in harmony with those of India's large landowners. Therefore, he expected that Jinnah would oppose the social reforms advocated by Gandhi oriented Congress. [24] Later in the post independent period Nehru was particularly careful in dealing with the Muslim politics. For instance, in Kerala, despite the support extended by Indian Union Muslim League to oust the Communist government in 1959 and the success of Congress – Muslim League-PSP alliance in the mid-term elections of 1960, Nehru did not approve the demand of the KPCC to bring the League in the coalition government. He feared a communal back clash in other parts of the country in the event of the Congress-League tie up, which would have brought gains to the Bharatiya Jana Sangh at the national level.

Similarly, Nehru's difference with the Union President Dr. Rajendra Prasad on the question of Uniform Civil Code is also well known. In fact, the Constituent Assembly Debates make it clear that Nehru wanted to implement it at a later stage so that the country becomes mature enough to accept and implement Uniform Civil Code. He was careful to see that the issue does not hurt the Muslim sentiment, especially when the vast majority of Muslims preferred to make India, not Pakistan as their mother land. Until the majority community shows a model for structuring their religious code into a uniform pattern it would be difficult for the country to implement the UCC. This position of Nehru was made clear to Dr. Rajendra Prasad, who raised serious criticisms of keeping the Uniform Civil Code in the part on Directive Principles of State Policy in the Constitution. After a series of debate and exchange of letters, Nehru finally asserted his constitutional role as the Prime Minister of the country. Despite the continuing differences, Nehru approved Dr. Rajendra Prasad's candidature ship in the Congress Working Committee for a second term as a President of India (although, he suggested that hereafter no serving president shall aspire for a third term).

According to Nehru, a communal movement was not religious, but that does not mean it was not have a religious background in India. It is exploited for political goals. "It is also economic in the sense that the political problem largely arises because of the problem of unemployment in the middle classes, and it is the unemployment among the middle classes that helps the communal movement to gain importance. [25] In fact, the Congress sincerely tried to reduce communal tensions during the period of freedom struggle. Many critics believed that the very concessions Congress made to the Muslim League had encouraged the League's quest for *territorial autonomy*. But Nehru viewed the widening rift between Muslims and Hindus as stemming primarily from political and economic, rather than religious differences. [26] His perspective was on scientific grounds and on this analysis we can observe a Marxist influence in his vision. Probably very few leaders of his time could hold a similar view in the Congress movement.

Socialist and Secular Ideas of Nehru

Nehru's extensive reading and exposure to the European Society had made him both a democrat and socialist. The influence of Fabian School of thought and developments in British politics had shaped his ideas on democratic socialism and parliamentary democracy. However, for the Congress movement, shift towards socialism was not an easy exercise. The radicals in the Congress clandestinely carried Marxian ideology whereas leaders like Nehru preferred a peaceful path towards socialism. Indeed, the Congress was not ready to evolve an ideological frame work for the organisation during 1920s and 1930s. Nehru's efforts began from here which he succeeded in emphasizing the significance of rational planning measures for a post- independent India (probably the efforts of USSR in shaping a planned and controlled economy appealed to him). The other great achievement was the amendment brought to the Party's Constitution, following the Avadi session of 1955 declaring the Congress's commitment to establish a socialistic pattern of society. Although, Communist leaders criticized this declaration, the later events had shown India's strength in structuring huge public sector, balanced movement towards a mixed economy, the role of the state in welfare sector, infrastructural developments and restricting the profit motives of private sector. The sound basis of a welfare state was thus provided in the initial phase of India's development.

Nehru saw socialism as a control of capital in national interest rather than as an imposition of authority on private enterprises. Political freedom was essential but, he held, "without social freedom and socialistic structure of society and the state, neither the country nor the individual could develop much. [27] In 1931, the Congress Resolution paid specific attention to economic programmes such as taxation, expenditure and economic policy. Jawaharlal Nehru played a very crucial role in getting these resolutions approved. Thus, the Karachi Resolution was an important land mark in the economic history of modern India and that was the first official Congress of pledge in favour of socialism. [28] Influenced by the Keynesian approach he believed that the economic activity was to be stimulated and regulated by *non-market* agencies, particularly the state. The relevance of Keynesian economics to the emerging post-colonial India was Nehru's revelation. [29] However, Nehru received strong opposition to his socialist ideals within the leadership of the organization. In an outspoken letter to Nehru, Dr. Rajendra Prasad, Sardar Patel, C. Rajagopalachari, Acharya Kripalani and other members of the Working Committee warned him at the end of June, 1936 in unambiguous terms. [30]

Although Gandhiji differed with Nehru, especially on the issue of large scale industrialization, on the question of leadership of the state, Gandhiji had no doubt in nominating Nehru as the leader of Congress and India. This is also a clear proof to Gandhiji's vision in estimating the future of India and Nehru's role as a modernizer. Looking back, if India had provided herself with a sound basis in most of the spheres and when neo-liberalization came in 1990s, by the time, three generations could derive the benefits of the state extended support. India's extra ordinary emergence in new-age industries–software, information technology and business process outsourcing–is the indirect result of Jawaharlal Nehru's faith in scientific education. [31] The state funded education mobilized Indian masses, although in proportion to population, it was small but the real impact was much more than it appears on the surface.

In fact, Nehru's ideas served as a bridge between democratic socialism of the Fabian type and Gandhian idea of Swaraj and welfare. He was convinced that "capitalism necessarily leads to exploitation of one man by another, one group by another, one country by another. [32] Hence, Nehru's conviction on socialism is very clear—"A democratic collectivism need not mean an abolition of private property, but it will mean the public ownership of the basic and major industries. Such a system of democratic collective will need careful and continuous planning and adaptation to the changing needs of the people". [33] Whatever be the criticism, the establishment of Planning Commission had provided a clear direction and responsibility on the part of the State in addressing the basic issues of the people.

We can notice a clear link between the ideals of planning and commitment to establish a socialist pattern of society. Unlike many post-colonial societies, which fell into the trap of *dependency syndrom*, India tried to develop a self-reliant economy. Nehru said, "Democratic planning means the utilization of all our available resources and in particular, the maximum quantity of labour, which is willingly given and rightly directed for good of the community and the individual. The growth of industry, both big and small is essential for any modern nation, indeed, without industrial development, there can be no higher standards for our people, no strength in the nation and perhaps not even our freedom can be preserved". [34] India is industrially more developed than many less fortunate countries and is reckoned as the seventh or eighth among world's industrial nations. But to remove this poverty by greater production, more equitable distribution is the paramount need and the most pressing task before us and we are determined to accomplish this task. [35]

An interesting blend of Socialism, Gandhism and welfare ideals could be reflected in these statements. Nehru was able to lead the Congress through the socialist path, without accepting communism, Gandhian path, though not appreciative of Gandhi's conception of state, and welfare ideas without aligning to the Capitalist ideology. Henceforth, given this situation, pro-capitalist leaders in the Congress party soon went out of the party. The launching of Swatantra Party in 1958 by leaders like C. Rajagopalachari, Piloo Mody and M.R. Masani to uphold the interests of the pro-capitalist class was therefore not surprising in Indian politics. Nevertheless, Swatantra Party did not gain much roots in the national politics and eventually merged with the Janata Party in 1977.

Nehru's famous epithet while launching the Bakhra Nangal Dam as the *temple of modern India* is another interesting contribution to the discourse on development. Nehru not only borrowed a concept from Indian tradition, but tried to integrate with the modernizing discourse of India. He never neglected the importance of agriculture in India's economy. The First Five Year Plan gave emphasis to agriculture. But it is sad to note that Congress was not able to achieve the goal of land reforms during Nehru's time or even thereafter. If the blame for not implementing land reforms goes to the state governments (being a state subject), can we ignore the fact that almost all states (barring Kerala) was under the Congress rule for a long time?

Indeed, Gandhi differed with Nehru on many vital areas. He was against rapid industrialization for an undeveloped society like India and instead advocated self reliance through cottage industries. Gandhiji commended in 1940 as follows— "Nehru wants industrialization, because he thinks that if it is socialized, it (will) be free from the evils of capitalism. My own view is that the evils are inherent in industrialization, and no amount of socialization can eradicate them. [36] Nehru, on the other hand, was influenced by the rise of welfare state in the West with liberal moorings. At the same time, he was very much sensitive to the post-feudal and pre-capitalist setting in Indian political system. As Prime Minister, he advised the workers not to waste their time and energy on strikes but to increase production, to enable the government to go ahead with its developmental schemes, aimed to raise the economic standards of the people. He differed with the Communists for using force and creating atrocities in the name of an economic doctrine. [37]

Despite the world of differences, Gandhiji understood Nehru and suggested him as his successor. He argued that Nehru could be the most idealistic, progressive champion of well-being of people....thus with the approach of independence, Jawaharlal quiet naturally was named India's first Prime Minister. [38] Earlier in a statement released on March 4, 1936, Subhash Chandra Bose also accepted the significance of Nehru's leadership—"Among the front rank leaders of today, you are the only one to whom we can look up to for leading the Congress in a progressive direction. More over, your position is unique and I think that even Mahathma Gandhi will be more accommodating towards you than any body else. I earnestly hope that you will fully utilize the strength of your public position in making decision. Please do not consider your position to be weaker than it really is. Gandhi will never take a stand which will alienate you. [39] Indeed, Subhash Chandra Bose was very prophetic in two senses—Nehru's succession to the mantle of Gandhi in Indian politics and Bose's sidelining by Gandhi in the Congress movement.

Although, Subhash Chandra Bose won the Presidentship of the Congress at Tripura AICC held in 1937 against Patabhi Sitaramayya, he could not go further because of lack of Gandhi's support. In fact, Gandhi resigned from Congress consequent to Bose's victory and the defeat of his nominee Patabhi Sitaramayya. Bose never came back to the Congress and focused his work on strengthening the INA. Gandhiji, on the other hand, did not renew his formal membership in the Congress, although in content and spirit he continued as the moral force to guide the Congress till his death in 1948. Nehru paid great tribute to Subhash Chandra Bose by accepting his salutation of the Indian Flag *Jai Hind* .Subsequently, all

Indians chant *Jai Hind* after singing the National Anthem.

Nehruvian conception of secularism was a blend of western and Gandhian ideas. As a rationalist, Nehru was a non-believer (his last will that after death, body may be cremated, and ashes may be poured in to Indian soil rather than keeping it for any religious purpose is good evidence). "Jawaharlal Nehru held to *secularism* as a tenet of the State, which ought to remain divorced from religion, though, of course, elements of *mild Nehruvian celebration of India's Hindu culture were allowed to mingle with that notion*". [40] He used religious idioms for communicating to the people on the national efforts to modernity since he found it an effective tool for political communication with the masses. On human deeds and actions, he believed in the law of nature rather than the scriptures of any particular faith. Indeed, Gandhian influences of *Sarva-dharma-Samabhava* and ideas of *Vasudeva Kudumbakam* had impacted on Nehruvian vision on secularism. In fact, it was his blend of secularism that got a prime space in the part on Fundamental Rights of the Indian Constitution. The Indian state has no religion but would not discriminate between a believer and a non-believer. Again minority rights are enshrined in Article 29 and 30 of the Indian Constitution. In the Constituent Assembly Debates on freedom of religion, Nehru's contribution is thus very conspicuous.

Despite the setback on certain fronts Nehru's contribution to the making of the foreign policy of India was remarkable. Although opposed to join Commonwealth unless British imperialism was discarded, as per the Lahore session of the Congress, his attitude underwent a drastic transformation in the post World War II scenario. [41] Actually, the grounding of India's foreign policy was laid down in the Congress meetings. In the later period, Nehru's impact in shaping foreign policy improved phenomenally. Nehru's control over the post-independent Congress Party's machinery and lack of a unified opposition outside the Congress resulted in his virtual monopoly in the field of foreign affairs. [42] Conversely,

Nehru and perhaps V.K. Krishna Menon had to take all the blames in regard to Kashmir problem and Chinese attack in October, 1962.

Congress as a Coalition

The unique coalition character of the Congress was a product of the synergy produced by the mass participation in it and the variety of regional leadership emerged in different parts of the country. The common goal of attaining freedom and the appeal of liberal nationalism brought the divergent sections towards the movement. Along with that, it was the task of the leadership to evolve demands and policy choices relating to the future of the nation-state, the Congress was going to create. Therefore, Congress debated on wide range of issues like planning and development, foreign policy, commitment to social reform and social justice, linguistic reorganization of states, approach towards native rulers, etc. It was not possible to create quick consensus on these aspects. Consequently, the factional character and diversity of ideas evolved inside the Congress during the early period itself. Being the successor of the movement committed to attain freedom, the Congress party had tremendous responsibilities in providing national unity.

Unfortunately,   even   during   the   Nehruvian   era, factionalism, regionalism, casteism and communal politics influenced the shaping of party democracy. A genuine liberal culture of democracy based on parliamentary traditions like in the West was not easy to evolve in the socio-economic context of India in 1947. Yet, being the sole national party, which could claim wide base among the people, the Congress tried to instil democratic values through organizational elections besides taking lead in national polls. Leadership succession, during those periods, was not linked to personality factor but based on larger consensus shaping inside the Congress party. Welles Hangen, (1963) in his work, *After Nehru: Who?* points out that Nehru left it to the wisdom of the CWC to decide on his successor after his death. When Kamaraj sounded the name of Mrs. Indira Gandhi, Nehru remarked, "Not Indu now, perhaps later". He was very well aware of the position and influence of the top ranking senior leaders of the party both at the national and state level. Being a democrat, he was not committing himself to dynasty politics. While confronting the issue of succession directly in a 1961 interview, he said, "I am not trying to start a dynasty. I am not capable of ruling from the grave. How terrible it would be if I, after all I have said about the process of democratic government, were to attempt to handpick a successor. The best I can do for India is to help our people as a whole to generate new leadership as it may be needed". [43]

Despite the objections, the Congress party had extensively used his reputation and personal influence for gaining electoral dividends on many occasions. Especially in the Third General Elections held in 1962, posters appeared across the country stating as, *Vote for Congress party and strengthen the hands of Jawaharlal Nehru.* He expressed opposition in making a demagogue out of himself. But when V.K. Krishna Menon, a close friend and associate of Nehru, was locked up in a contest in Bombay, he personally campaigned in the constituency and tried to disarm the regional politicians who were raising localism against Menon. At one point, Nehru emotionally appealed to the masses that defeating Krishna Menon will be considered as a defeat for Nehru himself. Of course, Nehru's appeal helped the victory of Krishna Menon. However, Krishna Menon was defeated in Bombay in the post-Nehruvian period. Eventually, Menon left the Congress Party.

Rajni Kothari's contribution of *Congress System* in Indian politics (1965) has significance beyond academic debate. The concept offered the idea that the Congress party had always possessed the flexibility and style to absorb dissent and opposition within its fold and this shaped a new style of democracy in the country. As a result of the operation of the *Congress System,* Opposition in Indian politics became very weak, until recently. The *Congress System* enabled the dissident politics to activate vigorously inside the party. The *coalition character* continues even today although the constituent elements of the coalition have changed over the period. The surge and decline of the party in the contemporary period is directly linked to the alignment and realignment of the constituent elements. The ideology of the party has also changed over the period. It had tried liberalism, democracy, socialism and now neo-liberalism, yet consistently maintained the values of a pan-Indian national party.

An Evaluation

Broadly, for convenience, we can divide the role and impact of Nehru on the Congress party into two clear divisions-during the movement era and post-independent era. During the former period, galaxy of senior leaders actively functioned with divergent and convergent views. In a way, Nehru enjoyed a distinct identity as a western educated and trained personality when compared to leaders like Gandhi, Sardar Patel and others. Yet, the leadership complemented and gradually evolved into a mighty nationalist force against imperialist authority. Again, Nehru considered Congress movement as more important than ministerial power during this phase. He even refused to contest elections held in 1936 based on Government of India Act, 1935. Despite his differences on many issues Gandhi nominated him as his successor and this itself is the testimony of Nehru's place in the freedom movement. Again, for all their disagreements, neither had doubted the others sincerity. [44]

The post-independence era was thick with many issues and developments. On the crucial hour of midnight to freedom, Nehru reminded all members of the Constituent Assembly that freedom and power bring responsibility. [45] Nehru's leadership was successful to a great extent in institutionalizing liberal democracy in a complex society. India's cherished goals of democracy, secularism, socialism and non-alignment were given a strong foundation by Nehru, although the last two had now reached a controversial stage, which was beyond the control of the present Indian leadership. Yet, contemporary India now focused on social justice and inclusive development as far as the directions of socio-economic development are concerned. Again, despite our alliance with western powers, India's commitment to peaceful relations with all the nations, faith in collective security and multilateral world order are of high significant value to day. Of course, Nehru's setback on Kashmir issue and Indo-China War in 1962 had been well debated in political history.

In the Congress party, the death of Sardar Vallabhai Patel on December 16, 1950 left a great void in leadership. Perhaps, Nehru lost a rival colleague which otherwise would have led to many political developments. Yet, it can be pointed out that there were many senior leaders who were not sycophants of Nehru and their critical role restricted him from committing major mistakes. However, Nehru had his own style and strategy. When ever, Nehru felt he could not have his way accepted in the party, he offered to step down. But then, other leaders would agree to accept Nehru's views. This was a pressure tactic Nehru used on more than one occasion as Prime Minister.

In the wake of Tandon-Nehru conflict in 1952, Nehru won, but was very careful in not asserting too much (he wrote anonymous article, criticizing himself during this period). The rise of Syndicate as an informal pressure group in the late 1950s also checkmated him. Some of the Congress Chief Ministers and PCC Chiefs defied him and on most issues he displayed democratic temperament. It would be a travesty of truth to blame Nehru for the creation of dynastic succession in Indian politics, if one would closely follow the developments that led to the election of Mrs. Indira Gandhi as Congress President for one year in 1959 and her elevation to the Prime Ministership in 1966 under different circumstances. Again, regular organizational election featured in the Congress party during Nehru's period.   This also justified the party's commitment to inner party democracy.

Another significant contribution was the role he played in institutionalizing parliamentary democracy in India.   He held the constitutional norms and parliamentary procedures in a dignified manner throughout.   His regular meetings with the head of the State and setting up of conventions were effective contributions.   Nehru's optimism on Indian politics was remarkable but with his death the country's social division rapidly worsened. [46] With the great split in 1969, the values of inner party democracy and collective leadership also began to decline in the Congress. Altogether one can say with confidence that both Congress as an institution and Nehru as a personality complemented each other. Neither could dispense with the other and it provided a fine tuning in political culture. Perhaps with the split in 1969, a great amount of Nehruvian values started depleting from the party. Hence, it is a debatable point as to how much we can estimate the Nehruvian legacy reflected in the contemporary political process of India.

Notes

1. Girish Mishra (1988), Nehru and the Congress Economic Policies, New Delhi, Sterling, p. 33.
2. Nandalal Gupta ed. (2006), Jawaharlal Nehru on Communalism, Gurgaon, Hope India Publications, pp. 259-260.
3. Edward Luce (2006), In spite of the Gods: The Strange Rise of Modern India, London, Little Brown, p. 194.
4. A.H. Somjee (1989), Political Society in Developing Countries, London, McMillan Press, p. 55.
5. Ibid., pp. 55-56.
6. Ibid., pp. 58-59.
7. S.R. Singh and M.B. Shrivastava (2004), Socio-Economic Ideas of Nehru and Globalization, New Delhi, Anmol Publications, pp. 35-48.
8. Mushirul Hassan ed. (2007), Nehru's India: Selected Speeches, New Delhi, Oxford University Press, p. 244.
9. Durga Das (2004), India: From Curzon to Nehru and After, New Delhi, Rupa Publishers, p. 267.

10. Edward Luce (2006), op cit., p. 220.
11. Jaswant Singh, (2009), Jinnah: India-Partition-Independence, New Delhi, Rupa Co., p. 155.
12. Stanley A. Kochanak (1968), The Congress Party of India: The Dynamics of One Party Democracy, New Jersey, Princeton University Press, p. 112.
13. Ibid., p.214.
14. James Manor ed. (1994), Nehru to the Nineties: The Changing Office of the Prime Minister of India, New Delhi, Penguin Books, p. 9.
15. Ibid., p. 23.
16. Robin Jeffrey, *The Prime Minister and the Ruling Party* in James Manor ed. (1994), op cit., p. 161.
17. Ibid., p. 165.
18. Stanley A. Kochanak (1968), op cit., p. 56.
19. Ibid., p. 68.
20. Ibid., pp. 175-176.
21. Seetharam Goel (1993), Genesis and Growth of Nehruism, Vol.I, New Delhi, Voice of India, p. 12.
22. B.D. Graham, *The Prime Minister and the Hindu Right* in James Manor ed. (1994), op cit., p. 189.
23. Shashi Tharoor (2007), The Elephant The Tiger and the Cell Phone: Reflections of India in the 21st Century, New Delhi, Penguin Books, p. 85.
24. Dorothy Norman (1965), Nehru the First Sixty Years, Vol.I, Bombay, Asia Publishing House, p. 37, 64.
25. Dorothy Norman (1965), op cit., p. 413.
26. Ibid., p. 549.
27. Purnima P. Kapoor (1985), Economic Thought of Jawaharlal Nehru, New Delhi, Deep and Deep Publications, pp. 11-12.
28. Ibid., p. 79.
29. Ibid., p. 198.
30. Jaswant Singh, (2009), op cit., pp. 210-211.
31. Shashi Tharoor (2007), op cit., p. 21.
32. Raj Kumar (2006), Modern Indian Political Thought, New Delhi, Arise Publishers, pp. 271-272.
33. Ibid., p. 274.
34. Mushirul Hassan ed. (2007), Nehru's India: Selected Speeches, New Delhi, Oxford University Press, p. 159.
35. Ibid., p. 245.

36. Dorothy Norman (1965), Nehru: The First Sixty Years, Vol. II, Bombay, Asia Publishing House, p. 50.
37. Ibid., p. 413.
38. Ibid., p. 291.
39. Ibid., pp. 561-562.
40. Jaswant Singh (2009), op cit. pp. 229-230.
41. S.J.R. Bilgrani, ed. (1992), Nehru, Indian Polity and World Affairs, Delhi, Kanishka Publishing House, pp. 14-15.
42. Alka Vijh, *Indian Foreign Policy: Nehru's Perspective* in Taufiq A. Nizam (2006), Jawaharlal Nehru: The Architect of India's Foreign Policy, New Delhi, Icon Publishers. p. 67.
43. Shashi Tharoor (2003), Nehru: The Invention of India, New Delhi, Penguin Viking, p. 195.
44. Benjamin Zacharia (2004), Nehru, Routledge Historical Biographers, London, Routledge. p. 174.
45. The Times of India, Bombay, August 15, 1947. p. 1.
46. Nandan Nilekani, (2008) Imagining India: Ideas for the New Century, New Delhi, Penguin Group, p. 17-28.

Reference

Welles Hangen (1963), After Nehru: Who?, London, Rupert Hart-Davis.

5

Nehru and India's Foreign Policy

K.R. Singh

Pandit Jawaharlal Nehru has left his imprint on multiple facets of India's policies, including foreign policy. Nehru's policies reflected his vision of India. It was that of a country with a long tradition and civilization, as also a country that was destined to find its new role as an emerging major power in modern world. It was that intrinsic sense of pride in what India was and what it is destined to be that inspired Nehru to formulate his policies, including foreign policy.

Nehru's foreign policies can be analyzed in three broad phases: pre-Independence, Independence (1947-1964), and post-Nehru period. Nehru's legacy is still a part of the decision making in the first decade of the twenty-first century.

Pre-Independence Phase

Developments in and around India since the end of the First World War had great impact on the shaping of India's foreign policy thinking. Indian National Congress was fully aware of these developments as seen from various foreign policy resolutions passed by it during that period. Nehru among others like Ram Manohar Lohia had a role in shaping the foreign policy during that period. Indian National Congress also developed close contacts with nationalist parties in other Afro-Asian countries and also with several of their leaders who were often invited to attend the Congress Party sessions.

Nehru himself had travelled widely including the Soviet Union. Also, his vision of history and contemporary world was clearly reflected in his books like the Discovery of India and the Glimpses of World History. This vision of Nehru as also his role in the Congress Party was crucial in shaping India's foreign policy after India attained its Independence.

Nehru and Independent India (1947-1964)

Several scholars have sought to analyse the theoretical formulation of Nehru's foreign policy. Was Nehru an idealist or a pragmatist? Was his policy an active one or a passive one? Was the concept of non-alignment a basis of foreign policy or an instrument of India's foreign policy etc.? An attempt will be made to examine some of them briefly and to asses them in the light of foreign policy in actual practice during the period 1947-1964.

There is no doubt that Nehru did have his streak of idealism. This can be illustrated by two examples. The one is his belief in the destiny of India as an emerging great power. That meant that India had to chalk out a policy that would allow it to retain the autonomy of decision making; an essential factor underlying his policy of non-alignment that he pursued despite great odds.

The second was his commitment to global peace; particularly comprehensive global nuclear disarmament. One could argue that it was not an idealist policy but emerged from his conviction that it was the only practical way to avert the nuclear holocaust and destruction of global civilization. He, therefore, applied that logic even to his country. Was his refusal to develop a nuclear bomb, despite his firm support to develop an independent nuclear technology for peaceful purposes including power generation, a part of that conviction? Did he believe that India could speak with greater moral right on global nuclear disarmament only when it did not become a nuclear weapon power? Was it the reason why he rejected the advice given to him by Indian nuclear scientists to go ahead and explode a nuclear device? That refusal created problem for India in the context of NPT and nuclear non-proliferation as is clear even now from the Indo-US nuclear power debate.

While there are illustrations of Nehru's idealism, one can

also give examples of his pragmatism. While refusing to join the Western military bloc, Nehru had no hesitation in joining the British-led Commonwealth. Besides giving India a place in the larger Anglo sphere, it also offered India access to military supply from Britain, which it would not otherwise have since Britain was an active member of the Western Bloc. Most of India's weapons till 1962 were from UK. Again, Nehru did not hesitate to appeal to the West when it was attacked by China in 1962. It obtained weapons from USA and even Israel. Afterwards, India also acquired weapons from USSR. Thus, one can argue that while Nehru did formulate his policies in idealistic frame-work yet, when occasion demanded, he could be very pragmatic.

It also needs to be noted that Nehru's policy was not as isolationist or a negative policy despite the prefix 'non' before it; like non-alignment. It was an active and outward looking policy, Nehru sought an Afro-Asian base for his foreign policy. That led to the South-South cooperation (the Bandung spirit) as also to the policy of non-alignment, which led to the foundation of Non-Aligned Movement (NAM).

In a way, Nehru's policy seemed to erode the likely power base of the upper powers, especially of USA, in the South and to that extent obstructed American strategy of using the South in the Cold War against the Communist Bloc. No wonder, John Foster Dulles, in the US Secretary of State, had termed the policy of non-alignment as immoral. USA was leading the crusade against the communist 'evil' and India had refused to join in that fight. The US policy of considering itself as a more crusader continues even now.

Two interrelated facets of Nehru's foreign policy need to be examined; concept of non-alignment and international instrument of diplomacy especially the NAM and the UN General Assembly. The concept non-alignment offered India a large enough base that was different from that offered by the two power blocs. Thus it offered the newly emerged states a choice, an alternate to the super power-led policy of dividing the world into two antagonistic power blocs. Non-alignment then offered them a new option to pursue an independent foreign policy. Nehru turned his concept of non-alignment of late 1940s into a policy in the fifties and an organization (NAM) by 1961 following the first non-aligned conference held in Belgrade. Nehru was not trying to play a balancing role between super powers. Rather, non alignment had an independent role outside the context of super power rivalry.

Associated with the concept of non-alignment was the concept of Afro-Asian solidarity. That meant that developing states could draw strength through operation among themselves. Also it gave them a sense of new identity from a colony to an independent state but delinked from its colonial past. The Bandung spirit symbolized that feeling. It was largely Nehru's personal magnetism and charm that could bring together diverse personalities with their own interests and agendas like Kwahma Nkrumah, Nasser, Tito, Sukaro, Bundaranaike etc. and knit them into a world force that expressed the demands and aspirations of the South at international level; be it the NAM or the UN General Assembly.

Major Issues of Foreign Policy

India, during the Nehru's era (1947-1964) faced several foreign policy challenges; four of them deserve special reference. They are the Kashmir question, challenges of 1954, the liberation of Goa (1967) and the 1962 War.

Kashmir question represented the unfinished agenda of the partition of British India and the accession of princely states. Three states posed challenges; Junagadh, Hyderabad and Jammu and Kashmir. Of the three Junagadh posed the least problem. The Nawab migrated to Pakistan and people opted for India. In Hyderabad the Razakar movement was posing a threat to the local population. The Indian forces, in a police action, quickly suppressed it. The Nizam preferred to stay and was made the Raj Pramukh.

The State of Jammu and Kashmir was the most different case. The Maharaja, for his own reason, delayed accession to either Pakistan or India. In the meanwhile the tribals and also Pakistani army personnel infiltrated into the state and posed severe challenge to life and property of the citizen. Maharaja was unable to control the events and ran away to Jammu where he signed the instrument of accession with India. Only then did India air lift its troops to Srinagar to confront the invaders. The immediate threat was averted but the solution still remains illusive.

Many questions remain unanswered. Could India have acted earlier or had it to wait for the formal signature to the instrument of accession? Would Lord Mountbatten, the Governor-General, have allowed military intervention by India without formal accession? Did India have to stop fighting and refer the question to the UN when reportedly it was on the offensive and gaining grounds? Who had advocated such a policy: the British, Sheik Abdullah or was that the result of Nehru's faith in the UN. Many of these questions remain unanswered even now and Kashmir continues to haunt Indian policy makers.

Challenges of 1954 were two fold - how to respond to the Pak-US military assistance pact, and how to contain the new threat in the north from a strong and resurgent China that forced even USA to accept a ceasefire in Korea.

It is necessary to put the events of 1954 in proper historical context. The US-Pak agreement has to be seen in the context of US policy of containing the Communist Bloc both politically and militarily. Thus it was expected that Pakistan would get not only weapons but also political backing of the West in its confrontation with India.

As far as China was concerned it still had close ties with USSR during the Stalin regime. Differences began only after the death of Stalin, the 20th Party Congress and due to the policies of the new team of Bulganin and Khrushchev since 1955. The break came only after 1962. Indo- Soviet relations during Stalin's period were, to say the least, unfavourable. Hence, India had to act on its own.

Thus, India's policy was to confront Pakistan militarily by acquiring arms mostly from UK and France, and to contain China through diplomacy of peace as reflected in the *Panchasheel* agreement that conceded Chinese position on Tibet but kept the frontier question open for negotiations. Did India have any other option? Some argue that India could have joined the Western alliances to confront China. That would erode India's insistence on following an independent policy; non-alignment. The *Panchasheel* dove tailed with non-alignment. Joining the West could have meant not only the end of non-alignment but also of South-South cooperation. Hence, it would have gone against Nehru's vision of India as an emerging major power.

Liberation of Goa in 1961 completed the unfinished agenda of national liberation and struggle against colonialism. While the French had agreed to a negotiated and peaceful decolonization so as to preserve their long-term political, economic and military interest in India, Portugal refused a negotiated settlement. Rather it reportedly sought to offer Pakistan military facilities in Goa. That would have posed a security risk. Portugal unlike France had no economic interests in India to protect. Also, decolonization in India would also mean giving up colonial empire in Africa. Portugal also believed that its membership of the NATO would protect it militarily. India thus had no other option but to liberate Goa, as also other parts in India, through military action. These operations were swift and smooth. India was criticized by the West but applauded in the Afro-Asian world.

The 1962 military debacle vis-à-vis China considered to be the great defeat of Nehru's foreign policy. That needs to be analyzed in more detail. The 1962 debacle had military and political reasons. While the Chinese were fully mobilized in Tibet and along the border, India was still struggling to build roads and other infrastructure to link the border up north with the foot hills. Reportedly troops were ill-equipped to fight a long war in those heights. Nehru-Menon team also had to make a hard choice between military advice and political demands. The army had reportedly argued for a strong defence near the foot hills where Chinese could be stopped and defeated rather than piecemeal distribution of troops along the route and spread along the crest. Krishna Menon reportedly argued against it and pursued the policy of defending the line at the border as claimed by India, the so-called Mc Mohan line, even with limited number of troops, the so-called forward policy.

Those policies though militarily a failure was politically correct. It allowed India to retain its claim to the border that it believed was its territory. Even a few Indian soldiers there symbolized Indian sovereignty. If they fight, they fight for the territory as Indians. If any had left that border unguarded and concentrate on defending the foot hills it would have politically surrendered the territory claimed by China to it even without fighting. Chinese would have occupied it and stayed put. Then Indians would have the hard task of attacking Chinese in that entire area. By pursuing a politically correct forward policy Krishna Menon lost the battle but Chinese had to withdraw beyond the line defended by the Indian soldiers with their blood.

Probably, Nehru and Menon believed that Chinese would not cross the border in such large force and if they did so the world would come to rescue India from the Chinese aggression. On both counts Nehru was proved wrong. He felt that he was betrayed not only by the Chinese but also by the world. Even the Afro-Asian friends 'medicated' rather than 'supported' India.

Probably India needed a 'lesson' on the intricacies of *sama, dana, danda, bheda* (of diplomacy of peace, of monetary inducement, use of force or coercion and of dividing the enemy and destroying the enemy from within) *Sama* (diplomacy of peace) alone can never be the basis of foreign policy. I think that we have still not learnt that lesson despite the experience of 1962.

The 1962 defeat or the slap on the face of India by the Chinese, undoubtedly a military strong power at that time, woke up India to the need for strengthening the *danda*. It gave a big boost to Indian defence preparedness. The defence budget went up from 2 percent to 3 percent of GDP. India raised new mountain divisions and acquired better artillery, tanks and aircraft. All these came handy when Pakistan decided to attack India in 1965. If India had not faced the humiliating defeat in 1962 and had not enhanced its military capability quickly thereafter, it would have suffered greater humiliation at the hands of Pakistan whose military strength had been further augmented by arms transfer from U.S.A. One should in fact thank the Chinese!

Science and Technology: Foreign Policy Dimensions

Nehru gave great importance to the development of science and technology in the context of his vision of India as an emerging major power. Since private sector was very weak at that time, public sector was entrusted with that task, besides the inputs in the educational sector like the opening up of various IITs. Thus, atomic energy, space, defence-related laboratories, DRDO, etc. were created and funded. Despite all the criticism, they paved the way for India to develop in the field of science and technology from the level of mid-eighteenth century to that of the twenty first century. It must be noted that many a times Indian scientists had to work under very adverse conditions due to multiple sanctions that were aimed at thwarting India's atomic and space/missile programme. That also affected other sector. It is ironical that these pioneers in science and technology that successfully faced the West in the past are being targeted by a section of Indians now for obstructing the growth of science and technology in India when they warn against surrendering to US on the nuclear power deal.

Nehru was against foreign dependence in science and technology especially in nuclear field. He is reported to have said, "If we depend too much on others for fissionable material, then inevitably that dependence will affect us in the sense that other people may try to affect our foreign policy, or any other policy, through that dependence." Nehru's concern about non/dependence on foreign support in the field of fissionable material is valid even today when India is being cornered to sign a nuclear deal on conditions that are seen by many scientists as a threat to India's national strategy.

Post-Nehru Era

There is no doubt that Nehru's framework of India's foreign policy continued to influence India's decision makers even after his death. Not only the Congress Party but others who had found faults with his policy formulations continued to quote Nehruvian model to accuse the government in power of transgressing from it. Interestingly, at least lip-services were paid to his model when India signed a Friendship Treaty with USSR in 1971. Today Nehru is quoted when India had developed a so-called strategic partnership with USA.

There is no doubt that both domestic and also international environment is changing rapidly. Yet, it is as important today, as it was in 1947, to reaffirm India's role as a major power, and that independence of decision making continue to remain as vital a part of foreign policy today as it was in the past. One hopes that those who claim that the world order is changing keep Nehru's basic postulates in mind while attempting to redefine India's policies in the years to come. In this context it is worth quoting Nehru.

"What does independence consist of? It consists fundamentally and basically of foreign relations. That is the test of independence. All else is local autonomy. Once foreign relations go out of your hands into the charge of someone else, to that extent and to that measure you are not independent". Something said four decades back is equally valid even today.

Are Indian policy makers, while paying lip services to Nehru, really adhering to this basic postulates of an "independent" foreign policy; hall-mark of a sovereign, independent state, and the basics of the policy of non-alignment.

6

Glimpses of Jawaharlal Nehru

L.C. Jain

'A moment comes, which comes but rarely in history, when we step out from the old to the new, when an age ends, and when the soul of a nation, long suppressed, finds utterance. The past is over and it is the future that beckons to us now'.
(Tryst with Destiny, Jawaharlal Nehru, August 15, 1947)

Nehru gave us glimpses of world history and came to occupy an honoured place in the history of the world. According to Sushila Nayyar, talking about Jawaharlal's *Glimpses of World History* Gandhiji said in November 1943 during his last imprisonment in the Aga Khan Palace that "if I were to sit down and write, I would feel happy to translate this book".

I understand the major objective of setting up the Nehru Studies Centre is to familiarize the new generation of students about the noble contributions if epoch making national leaders like Jawaharlal Nehru. The Centre will also conduct elective courses on Nehruvian ideas such as on Planning, Socialism, Democracy, Secularism, and Non-Alignment. Teaching materials are to be prepared along with fieldwork and action research.

Let me to recall my own journey where I had opportunity of being with or working with Nehru on various public issues, events, activities on different occasions. Such an account, I hope may suggest some fruitful areas for revisit by this Centre. The journey will start with my days in the students' movement during the freedom struggle and the Asian Relations Conference 1946-47 during the tenure of the provisional government i.e. pre-Independence.

The idea of such a conference was initiated by Nehru in 1946. It was organized at his instance by the Indian Council of World Affairs through a special organising committee headed by Sarojini Naidu and with Nehru as a member of the Committee along with a galaxy of national leaders and scholars. I was a student of Delhi University in 1946 and was inducted by Mrs. Naidu as Assistant Secretary to the Asian Relations Conference along with Rajkrishna. Thus for about six months we came in very close contact with Nehru.

Nehru had underscored that freedom was indivisible–and though India's Independence was in sight, India will not rest so long as there was any country or people ruled by a colonial power. He especially cited Indonesia then under Dutch occupation.

Welcoming the delegates, Nehru said: "Friends and fellow Asians: What has brought you here, men and women of Asia? Why have you come from the various countries of this mother continent of ours and gathered together in the ancient city of Delhi?

"We stand at the end of an era and on the threshold of a new period of history. Standing on this watershed which divides two epochs of human history and endeavour, we can look back on our long past and look forward to the future that is taking shape before our eyes. Asia, after a long period of quiescence, has suddenly become important again in world affairs. If we view the millennia of history, this continent of Asia, with which Egypt has been so intimately connected in cultural fellowship, has played a mighty role in the evolution of humanity. It was here that civilization began and man started on his unending adventure of life. Here the mind of man searched unceasingly for truth and the spirit of man shone out like a beacon which lightened up the whole world."

"This dynamic Asia from which great streams of culture flowed in all directions gradually became static and unchanging. Other people and other continents came to the fore and with their new dynamism spread out and took possession of great parts of the world. This mighty continent became just a field for the rival imperialisms of Europe, and Europe became the centre of history and progress in human affairs."

"A change is coming over the scene now and Asia is again finding herself. We live in a tremendous age of transition and already the next stage takes shape when Asia takes her rightful place with the other continent".

The Conference and Nehru's address to its delegates is a rich source for researchers today. Recall India and China came face to face at that Conference. They also set up an Asian Relations organization. (See Nehru's notes on "Chinese Attitude to the Asian Conference"; and on "Asian Relations organization in Selected Works of Nehru", Second Series 2). Much water has flown since under and over that bridge in the past 60 years. This is a very pertinent and promising area of enquiry - what has happened in Asia, India-China interface, Burma, why, and what is in store for the future.

In August 1947 came Independence and with that the blood soaked partition. Partition led to massive migration of millions of people and Nehru called for immediate relief to prevent chaos and rehabilitation overtaking the country. Congress party was called to duty. I was sucked by AICC into refugee relief and rehabilitation as a volunteer, for a good eight years and that was the end of my stay at the University. But, a lot of learning flowed in from real life. Here too I was often close to Nehru – in relief camps, cooperative farms organised for landless refugees and specially resettlement of Frontier refugees at Faridabad through community efforts.

Then came the inspiring objectives of the Constitution–draft introduced by Nehru in December 1946 in the Constituent Assembly. The resolution envisaged an independent democratic Republic of India that would be a federal polity with residuary powers vesting in the autonomous units and sovereignty belonging to the people. 'Justice–social, economic and political; equality of status, of opportunity and before the law; freedom of thought, expression, belief, faith, worship, vocation, association and action' were to be guaranteed to all the people along with 'adequate safeguards' to 'minorities, backward and tribal areas and depressed and other backward classes'.

To recall some of Nehru's words: "It was not a mere form of words that I placed before the House, carefully chosen as those words were. But those words and the resolution represented something far more; they represented the depth of our being; they represented the agony and hopes of the nation coming at last to fruition. As I stood here on that occasion I felt the past crowding round me and I felt also the future taking shape. We stood on the razor's edge of the present, and as I was speaking. I was addressing not only this Hon'ble House, but the millions of Indians who were vastly interested in our work. And because I felt that we were coming to the end of an age, I had a sense of our forebears watching this undertaking of ours and possible blessing it, if we moved aright, and the future, of which we became trustees, became almost a living thing, taking shape and moving before our eyes. It was a great responsibility also to be inheritors of the great past of ours. And between that great past and the great future which we envisage, we stood on the edge of the present and the weight of that occasion, I have no doubt, impressed itself upon this hon'ble House".

"This resolution will not feed the hungry or the starving, but it brings a promise of many things—it brings the promise of freedom, it brings a promise of food and opportunity for all".

"We shall frame the constitution, but does anyone in this House imagine that, when a free India emerges, it will be bound down by anything that even this House might lay down for it? A free India will see the bursting forth of the energy of a mighty nation. What it will not consent to be bound down by anything? Some people imagine that what we do now may not be touched for ten years or twenty years; if we do not do it today, we will not be able to do it later. That seems to me a complete misapprehension. I am not placing before the House what I want done and what I do not want done, but I should like the House to consider that we are on the eve of revolutionary changes, revolutionary in every sense of the word, because when the spirit of a nation breaks its bounds, it functions in peculiar ways and it should function in strange ways. It may be that the constitution, this House may frame, may not satisfy that free India. This House cannot bind down the next generation, or the people who will duly succeed us in this task. May the time come when in the words of this resolution; this ancient land attains its rightful and honoured place in the world and makes its full and willing contribution to the promotion of world peace and the welfare of mankind".

But there were also reservations on some aspects of that draft, expressed by other members of the Constituent Assembly for example Prof. NG Ranga. "I am sorry to find that the members of the Drafting Committee have completely forgotten the very fundamental thing that was really responsible for bringing this Constituent Assembly into existence and for giving them this chance of drafting this Constitution for India. One would have thought that it would be their elementary duty to have suggested to us that this constitution is being framed by the Constituent Assembly which has been brought into existence by the labours of the countless martyrs and freedom fighters in this country guided and led by Mahatma Gandhi, but not a word has been said in regard to this matter". What is the scenario now after sixty years?

"I wish to remind the House, sir, of the necessity for providing as many political institutions as possible in order to enable our villagers to gain as much experience in democratic institutions as possible and in order to be able to discharge their responsibilities through adult suffrage in the new democracy that we are going to establish. Without this foundation stone of village panchayats in our country, how would it be possible for our masses to play their rightful part in our democracy?"

Let us recall the final words of Dr. Rajendra Prasad, President of the Constituent Assembly:

If the people who are elected are capable and men of character and integrity, they would be able to make the best even of a defective Constitution. If they are lacking in these, the Constitution cannot help the country. After all, a Constitution like a machine is a lifeless thing. It acquires life because of men who control it and operate it, and India needs today nothing more than a set of honest men who will have the interest of the country before them." (Rajendra Prasad, Concluding Speech at the Constituent Assembly by the Assembly President, November 26, 1949).

See references to decentralization later in this text; as well as the following sources:

Let us take the report of the States Reorganization Commission (SRC), especially its concerns on financial and development issues. It especially highlighted the consequences of *non-reorganisation* of Uttar Pradesh in a separate note by SRC chairman Sardar KM Pannikar.

"The position of Uttar Pradesh in the Union of India is something which no one interested in the reorganisation of the States of India can legitimately overlook. In population the Uttar Pradesh is nearly equal to Andhra, Telengana, Karnataka and Kerala put together, larger than the combined population of the Punjab, Rajasthan and the new Madhya Pradesh (including Mahakosal, Vindhya Pradesh, Madhya Bharat and Bhopal). Too great a disparity is likely to create not only suspicion and resentment but generate forces likely to undermine the federal structure itself but thereby be a danger to the unity of the country".

"If one were realistic and took into consideration the manner in which governments functioned all over the world, it would be easy to see that this preponderant influence which would accrue to a very large unit could be abused, and would in any case be resented by all the other constituent units. Modern governments are controlled, to a greater or lesser extent, by party machines, within which the voting power of a numerically strong group goes a very long way. It is also undeniable that there is a natural tendency for the representatives of a state to form or to be brought together into such a powerful political bloc. The real issue, therefore, is whether it is desirable to place any unit in a position to exercise an unduly large measure of political influence".

"One of the commonest arguments advanced before us by leaders in Uttar Pradesh was that the existence of a large, powerful and well-organised state in the Gangetic Valley was a guarantee for India's unity; that such a state would be able to correct the disruptive tendencies of other states, and to ensure the ordered progress of India. The same idea has been put to us in many other forms such as that Uttar Pradesh is the "back bone of India", the centre from which all other states derive their ideas and their culture etc. It is not necessary to examine these claims seriously for nothing is more certain to undermine our growing sense of unity than this claim of suzerainty or paramountcy by one state over others".

More than fifty years have elapsed since. There is much to learn as to what has happened.

Planned economic development has been a dynamic factor in post Independent India thanks to Nehru's imagination and drive. Nehru convened the first National Planning Conference on April 25, 1950 and underscored 'The Necessity of Planning'. It was a joint conference of the Planning Commission which had just been set up under Nehru's Chairmanship and the Planning Committee set up by the Congress Working Committee with Govind Ballab Pant as Chairman. "The Conference was meant to attempt synthesis of popular and official approaches in the Country's problems including raising of levels of production and employment and repair of the damage caused to the Country's economy by the

Second World War and by partition".

Incidentally, following the conference, there was an exchange of letters (May 25/26 1950) between Nehru and Sardar Patel who felt that "the functions of the Planning Commission vis-à-vis the executive machinery had to be clearly defined if embarrassments and entanglements were to be avoided". (Selected Works Second Series, Volume 14, part B).

Special instruments were forged for the purpose of planning namely the National Development Council (NDC) and the Planning Commission, which also became vital meeting points for the Centre and the states to steer together the national economy.

When the Planning Commission was set up in 1950 to initiate planned economic development, its Terms of Reference included among others 'ensuring adequate means of livelihood' as envisioned in Article 39 of the Directive Principles of State Policy. Official records tell us the rest of the story.

Recorded minutes of the early meeting of the National Development Council (NDC) and its Standing Committee show the concern at the highest levels about ending unemployment.

The object of a plan is to raise the standard of living of the people which could be done partly by utilizing the unutilized capacity but essentially by installing more machines and equipment, i.e. in other words, by increased investment. Mahalanobis pointed out that increased investment would result in the creation of new demands for consumer goods such as cereals, sugar, etc. It will also lead to an increase in employment, though the magnitude of employment opportunities would depend upon the nature of industries in which investment was made. Mahalanobis said that while we want to produce more machines, we must not ignore the small industries but should distribute the investment among different types of industries in a balanced manner so as to create as much employment as possible.

The Chairman then took up the next item regarding employment situation in the country.

Initiating the discussion Sh. G.L Nanda (Deputy Chairman of the Planning Commission) said that it was not possible to say with precision what the volume of unemployment or under employment in the country was at a particular time. This was a serious handicap. It was also not possible to say to what extent the position had improved or worsened during any specified period in an accurate manner. According to the information available, there had been no improvement in the employment situation as a whole. Referring to the statistics collected by employment Exchanges in respect of urban areas, Sh. Nanda pointed out that there had been a continuous increase in the number of the live registers even though the number of vacancies notified had also been rising. The States had been asked to make their own assessment and they were keeping the situation under review. Reports from States showed that in almost all Part 'A' States the employment situation—both in the urban and rural areas—had deteriorated except in Punjab where a slight easing in the rural unemployment had been reported as a result of large scale expenditure under the Plan.

Mahalanobis stated that it would be possible to institute a system of surveys over the whole country to find out whether there was some improvement or deterioration in the employment situation.

D.R. Gadgil observed that, in terms of absolute allotment, agriculture, industry and social overheads etc. should receive more. There should be greater emphasis on employment and from this point of view the increase in consumer goods should, as far as possible, be through the small scale and cottage industries. The term *Common production programme* was intended to cover both the machine and the hand sector.

In reply to an inquiry from the Chairman it was stated that the number of jobs which could be created with 3 percent or 5 percent increase in the national income were dependent also upon the pattern of investment. The employment component of heavy industries was low while it was high in the case of small scale and cottage industries.

In reply to another query from the Chairman as to the period in which it would be possible to deal with the unemployment problem on the basis of a five percent increase (in national income), *Mahalanobis stated that if hand industries could be activated, the fear of unemployment could disappear during a period of five years* (**emphasis added**).

In the 'General Approach of the Second Plan Frame', Mahalanobis reiterated that "the Chief aim of planning in India is to solve the unemployment problem as quickly as possible." There was also at hand resolute political will. Nehru told Parliament:

Our objective is (to) strive with all our strength for our planned development and trying to ensure progressively a more equitable distribution, and thus to raise the standards of the great mass of our people.

The plan of development has to be implemented whatever the sacrifice to bring relief and prosperity to the millions of our countrymen who have suffered for so long from the curse of poverty.

Attachment I

Government of India's Resolution setting up the Planning Commission, GOI, Cabinet Secretariat Resolution (Planning), New Delhi, the March 15, 1950.

1. For some years past, the people of India have been conscious of the importance of planned development as a means of raising the country's standard of living. This consciousness found expression in the appointment in 1938 of the National Planning Committee by the Indian National Congress. The work of the Committee was, however, interrupted by political and other developments in the beginning of the war, although much useful material has since

been published. In 1944, the Government of India established a separate Department of Planning and Development and at its instance, the Central as well as the Provincial Governments prepared a number of development schemes to be undertaken after the war. Problems of planning were reviewed towards the end of 1949 by the Advisory Planning Board which was appointed by the Interim Government of India, an important recommendation of the Board being the appointment of a Planning Commission to devote continuous attention to the whole field of development, so far as the Central Government was concerned with it.

2. During the last three years, the Centre as well as the Provinces have initiated schemes of development, but experience has shown that progress has been hampered by the absence adequate co-ordination and of sufficiently precise information about the availability of resources. With the integration of the former Indian States with the rest of country and the emergence of new geographical and economic facts, a fresh assessment of the financial and other resources and of the essential conditions of progress has now become necessary. Moreover, inflationary pressures inherited from the war, balance of payments difficulties, the influx into India of several million persons displaced from their homes and occupations, deficiencies in the country's food supply aggravated by partition and a succession of indifferent harvests, and the dislocation of supplies of certain essential raw materials have placed the economy under a severe strain. The need for comprehensive planning based on a careful appraisal of resources and on an objective analysis of all the relevant economic factors has become imperative. These purposes can best be achieved through an organization free from the burden of the day-to-day administration, but in constant touch with the Government at the highest policy level. Accordingly, as announced by the Honourable Finance Minister in his Budget speech on the February 28, 1950, the Government of India have decided to set up a Planning

Commission.

3. The Constitution of India has guaranteed certain Fundamental Rights to the citizens of India and enunciates certain Directive Principles of State Policy, in particular, that the State shall strive to promote the welfare of the people by securing and protesting as effectively as it may a social order in which justice, social economic and political, shall inform all the institutions of the national life and shall direct its policy towards securing, among other things:

- that the citizens, men and women, equally, have the right to an adequate means of livelihood;
- that the ownership and control of the material resources of the community are so distributed as best to subserve the common good; and
- that the operation of the economic system does not result in the concentration of wealth and means of production to the common detriment.

4. Having regard to these rights and in furtherance of these principle as well as of the declared objective of the Government to promote a rapid rise in the standard of living of the people by efficient exploitation of the resources of the country, increasing production, and offering opportunities to all for employment in the service of the community.

The Planning Commission will:

- make an assessment of the material, capital and human resources of the country, including technical personnel, and investigate the possibilities of augmenting such of these resources as are found to be deficient in relation to the nation's requirements;
- formulate a Plan for the most effective and balanced utilization of the country's resources;
- on a determination of priorities, define the stages in which the Plan should be carried out and propose the allocation of resources for the due completion of each stage;
- indicate the factors which are tending to retard economic development, and determine the conditions which, in view

of the current social and political situation, should be established for the successful execution of the Plan;

- determine the nature of the machinery which will be necessary for securing the successful implementation of each stage of the Plan in all its aspects;

- appraise from time to time the progress achieved in the execution of each stage of the Plan and recommend the adjustments of policy and measures that such appraisal may should to be necessary; and

- make such interim or ancillary recommendations as appear to it to be appropriate either for facilitating the discharge of the duties assigned to it, or on a consideration of the prevailing, economic conditions, current policies, measures and development programmes; or on an examination of such specific problem as may be referred to it for advice by Central or State Governments.

References

Devaki Jain, (2005) Women, Development, and the UN: A Sixty-Year Quest for Equality and Justice, New York, IUP.

Government of India, (1955) Report of the States Reorganization Commission.

Government of India, (1978) Report of the Committee on Panchayati Raj Institutions, Asoka Mehta Committee, Ministry of Agriculture and Irrigation, Department of Rural Development.

JNMF,(1984) Nehru on Asian Relations Conference, Selected Works of Jawaharlal Nehru, Second Series, Volume Two, A Project of the Jawaharlal Nehru Memorial Fund.

L.C. Jain (2001), Our Constitution, Social Order & Environment, What is their night soil carrying capacity, Parisar Annual Lecture.

——LC Jain with BV Krishnamurthy and PM Tripathi, (1985) Grass without Roots: Rural Development under Government Auspices, Sage Publication.

——LC Jain and Karen Coelho, (1996) In The Wake of Freedom: India's Tryst with Cooperatives, Concept Publishing Company.

——(1998), The City of Hope: The Faridabad Story, Concept Publishing Company.

———Women are on the rise, but it's '33 percent vs. 66 percent, The Asian Age, 13 August 2005.

———58 years of freedom? Think of the dirt-poor, The Asian Age, 20 August 2005.

———Civil rights get buried under criminal neglect, The Asian Age, 3 September 2005..

———Akshara's preschools raise the drop-in rate, The Asian Age, 14 May 2005.

———Kundapur children revolutionise planning and police, The Asian Age, 21 May 2005.

———Why women in AP call arrack a killer, The Asian Age, 29 June 2005.

———Healthcare for all remains a distant dream, The Asian Age, 10 September 2005.

Oath administered by Gandhiji to Nehru and his cabinet colleagues in September 1946 – at dawn prior to assumption of office in the Provisional Government preceding Independence, Pyarelal Mahatma Gandhi, The last Phase, Navajivan Publications

Planning Commission, November (1957), Report of the Team (Balvantrai Mehta Committee) for the Study of Community Projects and National Extension Service, Vols. 1, 2 & 3, Committee on Plan Projects.

Reserve Bank of India (1981), Report of the Committee to Review arrangements for Institutional credit for Agriculture and Rural Development (CRAFICARD), Bombay.

Subhash C Kashyap, (1998), Resolution on Objectives of the Constitution, moved by Jawaharlal Nehru in the Constituent Assembly: 100 Best Parliamentary Speeches 1947-1997, Harper Collins Publishers.

Sushila Nayyar (1996), Mahatma Gandhi's Last Imprisonment – The Inside Story, Sushila Nayyar, Har-Anand Publications.

7

The *Menonian* Influence on *Nehruvian* Foreign and Security Policy

M.J. Vinod

In the realm of foreign policy, Nehru did not 'entirely' depend on his personal judgment. Depending on the event and circumstances on the ground, Nehru fell back for advice on a number of individuals. Lord Mountbatten for example played an important role at that stage, in working towards strengthening India's ties with the Commonwealth of Nations. Others included Madame Vijayalakshmi Pandit, Dr. Sarvepalli Radhakrishnan, Maulana Azad and K.M. Panikkar. Overshadowing all of them since 1954 was perhaps V.K. Krishna Menon. Nehru's relatively high opinion of Menon those days seemed to be backed up by Stafford Cripps and Louis Mountbatten.

In the words of Michael Brecher "no other Minister other than Krishna Menon concerned himself with the political aspects of foreign affairs, except in very special instances— Maulana Azad on Pakistan and the Middle East, and Azad and Pandit Pant on Hungary in 1956". Menon's rise to pre-eminence was meteoric. In 1938 Menon had accompanied Nehru on his European tour and since then the friendship blossomed. He even edited some of Nehru's books that were later published. He gradually emerged as the carrier of Nehru's views the world over, a role that was almost akin to that played by Harry Hopkins for President Roosevelt. After a rather lengthy period as head of the India League in London, he was appointed the first High Commissioner of free India to the United Kingdom. Since 1953 he led India's delegation to the annual sessions of the United Nations General Assembly, and served as Nehru's personal ambassador at many international conferences. In 1956 he became the Minister of Defence.

T.J.S. George, biographer of Krishna Menon observes that 'Menon burst on the world scene suddenly and dramatically soon after the country gained independence'. From then on for fifteen years he made everyone conscious of his presence: as India's High Commissioner in London immediately after independence, then as member of the Central Council of Ministers, first as Minister without portfolio and then as the country's Defence Minister. Menon was for the first   fifteen years after independence, always in the news both in India and abroad. Ultimately after the China debacle he was removed from office ironically through the 'efforts' of some of his own colleagues and party members.

Very few ministers other than Krishna Menon had concerned themselves with the political aspects of foreign policy making. Special circumstances that warranted inputs from other ministers included Maulana Azad in the context of developments in Pakistan and the Middle East. Both Azad and Govind Ballab Pant came into the limelight during the Hungarian crisis in 1956. Krishna Menon was Nehru's right-hand man in foreign policy matters for many years, though it may not be proper to exaggerate Menon's influence on the fundamental character and direction of India's foreign policy. Perhaps Menon would not have taken Indian foreign policy in a different course, even if he had the authority to do so. The Nehru-Menon axis can be looked at from the following areas and perspectives.

India and the Commonwealth

On March 11, 1948 British Prime Minister Attlee raised the issue privately with Nehru. He suggested that India remain within the Commonwealth and accept common allegiance to the Crown. In Attlee's view India did not have a common tradition of republicanism, which according to him was basically an importation from the West.

On the issue of accepting the King as the fountain of honour, Krishna Menon came up with the ingenious idea of 'dual sovereignty'. According to Menon, India would assert all its sovereign rights, but permit the King to exercise some of them. But even these proposals were rather unexpected and unacceptable to India. Krishna Menon was as anxious as any British statesman for India's continued association with the Commonwealth. As a compromise Krishna Menon suggested that India need not undertake any overt act of recognizing the King, but he could continue to be the President, as it were, of the club in which India would remain a member.

Nehru agreed India would neither recognize nor repudiate the King. There would be no mention of the King as the fountain of honour. Moreover the Commonwealth would not be perceived as some sort of super-state, but an association of free and independent states. [1] Finally India accepted the King as the 'symbol' of the free association of independent member states. The idea of the King being made the President of India was dropped. The Commonwealth also widened the platform on which India could play an international role, without any commitment to a bloc. Membership of the Commonwealth would in no way restrict India's freedom of action.

Korean War and Nehru: Krishna Menon Equations

The Korean War (1950-1953) as a case study in Nehru-Menon relations is indeed fascinating from a variety of perspectives surrounding the nature, course and India's role during and after the war. Patel accepted the two important resolutions passed by the UN Security Council. But this weakened India's leverage with the Communist powers, Russia and China. Nehru's position became rather insecure, particularly because Krishna Menon rejected the Government's Korean policy. He even offered to resign on this issue. In the words of S. Gopal:

"Nehru found his cluster of powerful ambassadors almost

an embarrassment for they began to display the 'disadvantages' of their eminence. Each pursued an almost independent foreign policy. Vijayalakshmi was eager to talk to President Truman, Krishna Menon met Attlee repeatedly, Panikkar saw himself as China's line of communication to the world, Radhakrishnan with his formidable personal image conducted his own private negotiations for peace with the Soviet Foreign Office and the American Ambassador in Moscow, and B.N. Rau at Lake Success assumed all too willingly, without waiting the approval of New Delhi, the leadership of the non-permanent members of the Security Council"

India refused to accept the US effort to link up the Korean Issue with Formosa and Indo-China. The US ignored the message passed on by Chou En-lai on September 21, 1950 through the Indian ambassador in Beijing K.M. Pannikar that "if America extends her aggression China will have to resist" because it would endanger China's security. In other words, Chou's message to the American's meant that, if the UN troops re-crossed the 38th Parallel, then China would enter the fray. This information was conveyed in turn to the US State Department by the Indian Ambassador in Washington. The response of the US officials surprisingly was that 'these Indians need not be taken too seriously, as they have played the game of the communists for long". The rest is now history.

Often India's role as a bridge-builder was misunderstood and even criticized. India's focus was to 'localise' the conflict and facilitate a peaceful end to the crisis. For doing this India often received raps on its knuckles. This represented the 'self-sacrificial' nature of Indian diplomacy during the crisis under Nehru. The war had bitter lessons not only for the participants, but also for peace-makers like India. The lesson for India was that it would not be prudent to go out of the way to help resolve a dispute, when its interests were not directly involved.

The Goa Episode

There is some evidence to suggest that Krishna Menon had

played a crucial role in persuading a 'reluctant Nehru' into using force ultimately to solve the dispute. Menon did convince Nehru to use force as Portugal was on the verge of 'internationalizing' the issue with the help of its friends and allies. It may be recalled that at that stage there was also a rumour that Portugal was 'secretly' negotiating a defence treaty with Pakistan. The implications of such a treaty on India's security could be well imagined.

Though the decision was painful and also represented a setback to his image, yet it had to be taken according to Nehru, in the larger national security interests of India. The alternative would have been a prolonged isolation for the people of Goa, Daman and Diu. Menon's role in silencing an 'angry' and 'hostile' western world is indeed noteworthy. When the western countries accused India of aggression, Krishna Menon retorted that "colonialism itself is permanent aggression".

India-China and Nehru-Menon Relations

The story of India-China relations since 1947, have been complex and controversial. Nehru broke the news of the border dispute to Parliament in September 1959 when he submitted a White Paper on Sino-Indian relations. Perhaps this was the first time that the public was informed by the government about the border dispute which had been in existence since 1954. All this happened during the chanting of *Indi-Chini bhai bhai*.

Nehru had come a long way since his talks with Prime Minister Chou En-lai for six hours on December 31, 1956 and January 1 and 24, 1957, following which Nehru had regarded Chou Enlai as a *brilliant man, one of the greatest he ever met*. By 1956 India was well aware of the road through Aksai Chin in Ladakh. By July and September 1955 the Vice Chief of the Foreign Bureau of Ngari (Western Tibet) had informed India's Trade Agent at Gartok of the Xinjiang-Gartok Road via Rudok. The Aksai Chin Road was built between 1951 and March 1957, when its completion was announced. The

Ministry of External Affairs held that *this part of the territory was useless to India... The boundary line had not been demarcated and had been 'shifted more than once by the British'. There was an old silk route which was a sort of international route. The Chinese had only improved it"* [2]

All this was known to Nehru when he met Chou En-lai on December 31, 1956. He did not mention the Aksai Chin Road even once in his talks with Chou En-lai. On the contrary Chou said that he accepted the McMahon line, he mentioned Tibet and assured respect for its autonomy. History was to later prove that none of them happened at least from the Chinese side. The Government of India, apart from a few angry condemnations, chose to ignore the strategic significance of Aksai Chin for long.

Krishna Menon as Defence Minister perhaps thought that he could handle China diplomatically. The Chinese Defence Minister in 1961 had told Menon that China would not attack India, and that he as Defence Minister trusted this statement. Hence Menon did not prepare the Indian army for a possible threat from China, or move forces swiftly when the occasion so warranted. The end result was disastrous. Hence after the war even influential members of the Congress party such as Mahavir Tyagi went to the extent of demanding the resignation of Krishna Menon in 1962. Since then Nehru was projected as a 'tragic hero' living through a 'terminal agony' from October 1962 until his passing away in May 1964. [3]

Following the war India had to face three core issues: coping with the immediate war situation and its aftermath; the fate of India's policy of non-alignment, and the need for acquisition of military capabilities for the longer term. [4] After the security debacle in 1962, Nehru opined that "our whole mentality has been organized by an approach to peace". In fact Nehru was never defensive about his 'idealism'. Often he used to say that today's 'idealism' is tomorrow's 'realism'. In a way, a final blow to India's pacifist thrust and its global role was delivered by the Sino-Indian war in 1962. At that stage India was spending a mere 2 percent of its GNP on defence.

Krishna Menon as Defence Minister

From 1957 to 1962 Krishna Menon held the post of Defence Minister. As a confidant of Nehru, Menon functioned as his alter ego for national security and defence planning. Hence the locus of decision making shifted from the 'cabinet' to the 'Defence Minister's Committee'. In a way Menon was responsible for laying the foundations of India's 'military-industrial' base. Menon was responsible for the establishment of various ordinance facilities. Some of these included the defence facilities to manufacture the 'Ichapore' semiautomatic rifle, a tank manufacturing facility at Avadi in Tamil Nadu, the Mazagon Dock naval shipyard at Mumbai to build frigates, and the licensed manufacture of Soviet-designed MIG-23 fighter aircraft in Nasik, Maharashtra.

In spite of these initiatives, there were many issues of contention regarding Krishna Menon. The most famous among them was the infamous 'Jeep scandal'. The scandal revolved around the purchase of jeeps for the use of the army, which the army had rejected due to their poor condition, but was forced to accept since the jeeps were already paid for. It led to the removal of Krishna Menon, who had fixed that deal while he was occupying the post of High Commissioner to the UK, following intense media and political pressure. But Nehru rewarded Menon with the post of Defence Minister with Cabinet rank. Soon after Krishna Menon took over as the Defence Minister, the government decided to drop the case slapped on the nondescript company that had supplied the jeeps.

The flip side to Menon was his idiosyncratic manners, his high-handed ways and his involvement in the 'tactical aspects of military decision making' at times did result in negative consequences. Hence his spat with General K. Thimayya when the latter tried to warn both Nehru and Menon about the emerging Chinese threat as early as 1959 was rather unfortunate. This even led to a head on clash and the resignation of Gen. Thimayya. Nehru was however able to persuade him to withdraw his resignation. In the Lok Sabha, strangely Nehru provided a rather weak defence of General Thimayya's action. Rather he sought to deflect the criticism targeted at the Defence Minister Krishna Menon.

Following General Thimayya's retirement as Chief of the army staff in May 1961, Menon appointed a relatively junior officer Lt. Gen P.N. Thapar to the post superseding a senior officer like Lt. Gen S.P.P. Thorat. This decision not only resulted in a rift between the 'professional military' and the 'political leadership. It also alienated many high-ranking officials in the Ministry of Defence, and tended to demoralize personnel in the civilian and military bureaucracies. S.S. Khera observes that when it came to the final climax, Krishna Menon found himself without friends anywhere, such as the top echelons of the military cadres and the civil servants in his own Ministry. It affected both their 'morale' and their 'will' to work together.

It did not help anyone, least of all Krishna Menon himself, for him to castigate the armed forces as a *parade-ground army*; however justified he thought he was in his judgment of the army. Krishna Menon was perhaps unable to realize at any moment the strength of the opposition against him. He had a deep conviction that he was right, and in this he remained unshaken to the very end. He also knew that he had Nehru's 'confidence' and 'support'. Ultimately the pressures against Krishna Menon simply became too much for even Nehru to manage. [5] The net result was the 'critical' gaps in 'defence preparedness and planning'. A strong perception exists that Menon's 'dominance' of the defence planning process significantly contributed to the military rout in 1962. In the context of the 1962 India-China conflict Nehru's attitude toward the military' his Defence Minister Krishna Menon perhaps further compounded the deficiencies' in India's military 'preparedness'. Nehru did concede that 'we are getting out of touch with the reality of the modern world, and living in an 'artificial world of our own creation'. Perhaps this comment affected the need to have a second look at the 'directions' of India's foreign policy.

The Indian defeat led to the establishment of a new Emergency Committee of the Cabinet. The Committee introduced a system of 'morning meetings' with the Minister of Defence and the three service chiefs. Often these meetings were conducted without a predetermined agenda, and to deal with contemporary defence issues on a regular basis. The meetings were also attended by the cabinet secretary, the defence secretary and the scientific adviser to the minister of defence.

The Flip Side to the Nehru-Menon Relationship

Krishna Menon constantly had maintained a barrage of denigration of Nehru's sister Vijayalakshmi Pandit, then India's High Commissioner in London – a post in which Menon had an inglorious innings –and attacks on "our Ambassadors...sniping at me", but also made innuendoes about Nehru himself. Finally Vijayalakshmi Pandit could no longer stand it and bitterly complained to her brother Nehru on February 5, 1957 about Krishna Menon. Nehru replies to her on February 13, 1957 as follows:

"You have referred to Krishna Menon and to various forces at work in London trying to discredit you. I think I am well aware of all this and, of course, strongly disapprove of it...I have known Krishna now for a long time and have a fairly good appreciation of his abilities, virtues and failings. All these are considerable. I do not know if it is possible by straight approach to lessen those failings. I have tried to do so and I shall continue to try. This is a 'psychological' problem of some difficulty and has to be dealt with, if at all successfully, by rather indirect methods. I propose to deal with it both directly and indirectly."

"I hope I have the capacity to judge people and events more or less objectively. I am not swept away by Krishna; nor would I like my affection for you to influence my judgment to any large extent, though to some extent, of course, affection does make a difference and indeed should. Krishna 'has often embarrassed me' and 'put me in considerable difficulties'. If I speak to him he has an 'emotional breakdown. He is always on the verge of some nervous collapse. The only thing that keeps him going is hard work'. There is 'hardly a person of any importance that he has not complained to me some time or other. Later he has found that his opinion was wrong and he has changed it. [6]

In spite of all this Nehru picked on Menon to deliver the harangues in the Security Council, during one of which he passed out, and also made him the Defence Minister. Vijayalakshmi contended that her brother knew nothing "of that other side" of Menon's character "which is in such complete contrast to the one you see". She believed that Krishna Menon's unpopularity was not so much due to his views on Suez and Kashmir, but due to what she termed his "twisted approach to problems and his manner of dealing with them". Nehru tended to ignore her advice.

Yet surprisingly Nehru wrote contemptuously of Krishna Menon to M.O. Mathai. In a letter dated September 29, 1951, he wrote "I saw a progressive deterioration till a time might come when he would disgrace himself not only before others but before himself...inner degradation and disintegration are far worse" than death. [7] The time did come. It was waiting to happen. The fact is Menon remained in office till 1962 thanks to Nehru.

Major Observations

It would be perhaps an error to exaggerate the 'Menonian' influence on the 'fundamental character' and 'direction' of 'Nehruvian' foreign policy. Nor is there evidence to suggest that even if Menon had the authority to do so, he would have steered the course of Indian foreign policy in any other direction. Though Menon was consulted on virtually all aspects of foreign policy, the extent to which he shaped foreign and security policy is difficult to say with any degree of clarity. Perhaps a distinction needs to be made between 'tactical' and 'strategic' decisions, and between the general policy goals and the specific details of negotiation.

Notes

1. S. Gopal. (1983) Jawaharlal Nehru: a Biography, Volume 2: 1947-1956, New Delhi, Oxford University Press.
2. A.G. Noorani, (2006) Nehru: Myth and Legacy (review article) Frontline, 23:2, January 28 – February 10.
3. Damodaran A.K., (1998) Jawaharlal Nehru: A Communicator and Democratic Leader, New Delhi, Radiant Publishers.
4. Nayar, Baldev Raj and Paul T.V, (2004) India in the World Order: Searching for the Major Power Status, New Delhi, Cambridge University Press.
5. Khera S.S. (1968) India's Defence Problem, New Delhi, Orient Longmans.
6. Selected Works of Jawaharlal Nehru: 1 December 1956-21 February 1957; Second Series, Volume 36, Jawaharlal Nehru Memorial Fund; distributed by Oxford University Press.
7. S. Gopal, op.cit, p.143.

References

Brown Judith M. (2003) Nehru: A Political Life, New Delhi, Oxford University Press.
Grigg, John, ed. (1992) Nehru Memorial Lectures 1966-1991, New Delhi, Oxford University Press.
Raman B. (2005). National Security Mechanism, Paper No. 1228, South Asia Analysis Group, January 24.
Tharoor, Shashi. (2003) Nehru: The Invention of India, New Delhi, Penguin Viking.
Wolpert, Stanley. (1996) Nehru: A Tryst with Destiny, New York, Oxford University Press.

8

Interpreting Nehru in the Context of India's New Foreign Policy

Rahul Tripathi

India's foreign policy in the recent times has been stated to . be driven by certain practical and pragmatic considerations which have led it to re-look at the issues and actors in global politics. While India has sought engagement and cooperation with partners which were for long kept on the margins of foreign policy because of ideological reasons, there has also been a clearer articulation of the factors that are likely to secure India's interests-political and economic. Such a clearer articulation of foreign policy objectives, though lacking in commensurate application on the ground, has definitely fitted well with India's emerging profile in the global scheme of things. In one of the most authoritative statements on the subject in the recent times, India's foreign policy has in the recent years has witnessed a definite shift from 'idealism to pragmatism'.

India's New Foreign Policy: The Debate

Under these circumstances, it is but natural that attempts be made as to in what way the 'new' foreign policy has been different from the 'old' one. Furthermore, seeking parallels and deriving value judgments based on the irrelevance of the old and remarkability of the 'new' have become very tempting exercises for scholars and analysts depending on which side of the fence they are. For once, the subject matter of foreign policy, which has always been reflective of a certain broad national political consensus in India, has also become a house divided. Ever since the change in India's national political formation in the late nineties, this debate has acquired political colours as well. A contrast is often seen between 'Congress foreign policy' and the 'BJP foreign policy'. Such a debate, though welcome in a democratic apparatus such as ours, misses a very crucial point. Foreign policies are always conceived and executed in a dynamic context. It always responds to and shapes the external environment a nation finds itself in a particular historical juncture which may not always be its own making. Any judgment of foreign policy therefore should be based on an approach, which studies continuities and changes in the policy rather than the regimes and their policies. In essence, foreign policy of a nation more than any other policy should be judged by the times and the circumstances in which it is conceptualized and implemented.

The present paper tries to reinforce this logic by taking Jawaharlal Nehru as a reference point. Nehru, as the builder of the idea of modern India, undoubtedly left his mark in varied aspects on policy making in India and very definitely on the foreign policy thinking in the country. It is therefore natural that Nehru provides the ideological framework from which continuities and changes in India's foreign policies can be dissected and inferences drawn on the ideological or pragmatic shifts if any. It first tries to go back to Nehru, his vision and Nehruvianism and then comes back to present to understand the shifts that have been evident in the recent times.

Nehru and Nehruvianism
Nehru was undoubtedly the architect of India's foreign policy in the post independence period wherein he not merely gave the ideological formulation of where India should stand, but he also tried to put into practice his own ideas of liberalism and freedom in the foreign policy arena. He was of a firm belief that India had to play a crucial role in establishing a just and moral world order, ensuring peace and cooperation across the globe. More than India's economic and political strength, it was her civilizational and ideological premises that gave her a

high moral ground in global affairs, he felt. Indeed, the Gandhian ideals on spiritualism and non-violence were deeply etched in India's role in global affairs that Nehru visualized immediately after independence. Non Alignment and Peaceful Coexistence therefore became the mantras of Nehru's foreign policies, which very often came to be labelled, perhaps rightly so as 'Nehruvian foreign policy'.

But Nehru himself was chary of the word 'Nehruvian' and was opposed to labelling such ideas as his own or to mark these policies as having his imprint. As Nehru insisted in a reply to a debate on foreign affairs in Parliament on December 9, 1958. [1]

"....it is completely incorrect ...to call our policy "Nehru" policy. It is incorrect because all that I have done is to give voice to that policy. I have not originated it. It is a policy inherent in the circumstances in India, inherent in the past thinking of India, inherent in the whole mental outlook of India, inherent in the conditioning of the Indian mind during our struggle for freedom and inherent in the circumstances of the case today. I come in by the mere accidental fact that during these few years I have represented that policy as Foreign Minister...I am quite convinced that whoever might have been the in charge of foreign affairs of India and whatever party might have been in power in India, they could not have deviated very much from this policy. Some emphasis might have been greater here or there because, as I said, it represents every circumstance that goes towards making the thought of India on these subjects ".

It is quite clear therefore, that Nehru contested the notions of the then foreign policy of India deriving its basic ideas from Nehru himself and therefore rejected the Nehruvian label to it. Secondly, the ideas that Nehru had were definitely shaped by the need for India to retain the autonomy of decision making when it came to forming opinion on global issues of concern. The essence of Non Alignment therefore appeared more a reflection of the moral principle of playing a major role on matters that divided nations on ideological matters. There was however at the same time a very pragmatic element in this policy as one could always judge the partners to choose as and when national interest required so.

At one level, Non Alignment, seen in a dynamic context was not a passive policy of staying aloof from global flashpoints, but it was rather the voice of dispassionate and independent reason. At the other level, it gave the member nations the option of judging their partners on relative merits. India's ability to maintain economic and political links with both the United States and Soviet Union in the some of the worst phases of the cold war is a clear manifestation of this logic. It is that engagement at both the levels in the past that provided the building base of what today stands as 'natural alliance' and 'strategic partnership'. Contrary to the popular perception that India was aloof and isolated because of Non Alignment, India was actively engaged with both the powers whether it was seeking military procurement from US after the Chinese debacle or entering into 'Treaty of Peace, Friendship and Security' with the Soviet Union at the peak of 1971 crisis. Such an approach would have been unthinkable had Non-Alignment not been made part of the official policy. Therefore, ironical as it may sound, the very criticism of Non-Alignment policy (that it was never practiced in reality) was its very success, one is inclined to believe.

Criticizing Nehruvianism: The Counterpoint

A more recent critique of Nehruvianism has been manifest in the foreign and defence policy literature in the nineties where India has seen a transformation in economic policies and realignment of political forces. As the two have more-or-less coincided, there has been the temptation to link the two. India's recent economic and strategic resurgence is seen as happening only after shunning the 'Nehruvian middle-path' and 'moral ambiguity' that was characteristic of India's foreign policy. While on one hand it is stated that India never had a strategic culture and was therefore devoid of a strategic foreign policy under Nehruvianism, some scholars see 1998 nuclear tests as the defining moment when India finally came to have a clearly articulated foreign policy that behoves a global power. It is therefore good for India that it sheds the Nehruvian baggage at the earliest, if it is to have a high seat of power in global politics, the suggestion is given.

A closer scrutiny of the dynamic approach to foreign policy and the role it plays in creating contemporary image of a nation would however suggest that the above arguments are misplaced and misdirected. India's emergence as a potential power in the nineties was an outcome of an incremental process rather than a sudden development. This incremental process had its roots in the times when India as a nation started rebuilding itself after independence, both economically and strategically. Obviously for a nation to have a grandiose foreign policy with delusions of a greater power would have seemed paradoxical given the monumental development challenges that India faced at that time. While maintaining a specific defence posturing would have been in order, there was a far more compelling need to focus on bringing the majority of people in the national economic and political mainstream. The Raj with its imperial resources and reach was never really known to have articulated a strategic foreign policy agenda for India despite some isolated voices on the contrary (Noorani). An independent India therefore could never be overnight expected to develop a strategic vision. If at all there could be a vision, it could only talk of India's pre-eminent location in the comity of nations premised on the ideals of peaceful coexistence and non-interference.

What began under Nehru was therefore a gradual process, which brought together like-minded nations and actors who believed that the challenges facing the Third World were common; therefore the steps to tackle them should also emerge from collective efforts. This guiding principle was reflected in the Asian Relations Conference and the early years of the Non

Aligned Movement. Over the years, however, there was a gradual movement from the idealistic and romantic phase to more realistic moorings as Nehru adjusted to political realities and emerging trends in world politics as well as the pressures on India born out of these trends.

Besides, it was only under Nehru that India saw the initiation of a comprehensive Nuclear energy programme which was later to provide the foundation for a full fledged nuclear weapons programme. It is widely believed that the legitimacy and sanctity that got associated with Indian nuclear programme had got a lot to do with Nehru's clear articulation of nuclear disarmament. Though, even as Nehru and its associates campaigned for nuclear disarmament, they appeared clear in their minds that India should not give up the option to make nuclear weapons in future. While it is true that a full-scale weapon development programme began only after Nehru's death, the incremental manner in which Nehru nurtured the nuclear establishment in the initial years speaks a great deal about the man's involvement with the issue. Coming out of the nuclear ambiguity in 1998 and conducting the tests was something that could only be done by a regime that had seen the nuclear policy and capability evolve over the years, certainly not by a leader who had sown the seeds of the same.

To denounce Nehru and Nehruvianism in the context of India's new foreign policy would be tantamount to discarding the very foundation on which the new policy is based. The author would like to contend that Nehru was both a realist and pragmatist when it came to the real world circumstances that India found itself in which were not always of its own creation. Just as India today is seen as responding to both positive and negative impulses generated from outside, similarly was Nehru responding and reacting to the world that India found herself in, perhaps more articulately than any other leader of his time.

Nehruvian Leadership after Nehru

After Nehru's demise, there was a definite vacuum felt in

the realm of foreign policy thinking and practice. While the leaders claimed to follow the Nehruvian legacy, they never had the stature to carry the legacy. India's foreign policy actions in the decades following Nehru therefore became more a reflection of episodic responses to particular situations rather than parts of a well thought out strategy for future. A fundamental deficiency in the Nehruvian legacy was that political leadership never really articulated a policy that could make India a determinant of changes in the region. Rather India became a factor in transforming scenario that surrounded it. India's commitment to Non Alignment and Third Worldism therefore became more of a ritual which was to be consummated during elaborate confabulations that went on during NAM and G77 meets in the seventies and eighties.

Nehruvianism nevertheless continued to provide the ideological background on which the Indian leadership based its policy pronouncements. Gradual work in p.ogress on the Nehruvian edifice was maintained, though at a more practical level, the rest of the world never really saw India as an emerging nation during those times. India was more a reflection of an idea which drew its sustenance from the past yet was not willing to adapt to the changing realities: a notion which literally ran contrary to the dynamic aspects of Nehruvian policy.

Nehru Revisits: Nineties and Beyond
It would therefore be very interesting hypothetical exercise to contemplate if Nehru was to revisit India's contemporary foreign policy and seek out the positives and negatives vis-à-vis his own thinking on the same.
1. Nehru would have certainly been pretty quick to accept the changes that world has undergone during the last twenty years and would have outlined long-term vision (which is at present lacking).
2. He would have been pragmatic enough to recognize the need for new partners and partnerships which would have

taken direct concerns of India's economic and security interests.

3. Nehru would have faced the dilemma of competing interests between a new ally and an old partner in a more pragmatic manner. He would have been less ambiguous than India's present leadership on how the Iran issue needs to be tackled.

4. Nehru would certainly have supported the coalition-building across developing nations in multilateral fora as that alone could have protected mutual interests.

5. Nehru would have been much more vocal on the present patterns of global domination and subsequent responses.

To conclude, Nehru's views and thinking on India's foreign policy continue to remain relevant not only because of the philosophical moorings they lead us to, but also because of a certain pragmatism that was inherent his articulation and practice. It is up to the present day leadership to convert Nehru's ideas into a greater political reality, if India has to acquire the same moral stature it enjoyed in the fifties and which it has certainly misplaced somewhere in its search for greater power.

Note

1. Iqbal Singh, (1992) Between Two Fires: Towards an Understanding of Jawaharlal Nehru's Foreign Policy, Delhi, Orient Longman, P.26.

References

A.G. Noorani Caroe's Lessons A Review of the book The future of The Great Game: Sir Olaf Caroe, India's Independence and the Defence of Asia by Peter John, Frontline, May 19, 2006.

Ashok Kapur, (2006) India: From Regional to World Power, London, Routledge.

C. Raja Mohan, (2003) Crossing the Rubicon: The Shaping of India's New Foreign Policy, Delhi, Viking.

J.N. Dixit, (2005) Indian Foreign Service: History and Challenge, Delhi, Konark.

M.V. Kamath, (2003) Nehru Revisited, Mumbai, Nehru Centre.

Venu Madhav Govindu, Nehru: A Contested Legacy A Review of the book Nehru: The Invention of India by Shashi Tharoor (2003)
http://www.indiatogether.org/2005/aug/rvw-inventind. htm

9

The Nehruvian Legacy: The Eternal and the Ephemeral in Foreign Policy

B. Ramesh Babu

Legacy is what our ancestors and parents leave for us. Heritage is what we make of it i.e., what we retain and reject, qualify and modify, and so on. The amalgam of the active constituents that guided us in the recent past, guide us at the present and in the immediate future is our *living heritage*. Naturally, the reigning cultural baggage of a nation contains many new ideas drawn from outside and other living cultures as well as several shaping forces emerging from the evolving collective experience of the people. It is not easy to disentangle the complex web of legacy, heritage and the new entrants and delineate their causal linkages to particular actions or ideas. It is in this broad context, an attempt will be made to look briefly at the Nehruvian legacy, with a focus on one of its key elements—the legacy of Nehru's foreign policy.

Pandit Jawaharlal Nehru and the pre and post-independent India were so intertwined that they cannot be separated. There is hardly an area of public life of the nation in those formative years that did not have his imprint --plus points, warts, and all. His pervasive influence and monumental impact was only second to that of the Mahatma. Since Gandhi fell to an assassin's bullet soon after Independence, Nehru towered over a whole generation of tall and truly great leaders. What an array of noble leaders were we blessed with! Rajaji, Sardar Vallabahai Patel, Pattabhi Seetaramaiah, Rajendra Prasad, Maulana Kalam Azad, Gurzari Lal Nanda and scores of others, who sacrificed their lives for their motherland and led the nation with dedication, sincerity and integrity—a rare and endangered species in today's India. Lal Bahadur Shastri was the last of the truly honest national leaders that lived amidst us and that was over four decades ago! Honest and self-sacrificing leadership certainly is the most glaring of the missing features of the legacies of the Nehru era!

Leaders by definition are those who lead people to goals and places where they would otherwise not seek or go. The goals sought were noble indeed: end of poverty and hunger, welfare of all the people, social justice, economic equality, and solidarity with the poor and oppressed people everywhere and the common good of the mankind as a whole. A strong streak of idealism was the driving force behind that legacy. This certainly is missing in our policies and actions in recent years. Just like many aspects of our public life today, the quality of our political leadership has degenerated beyond measure. What we have today mostly are leaders, who are the followers of their following! In the rat race to hold on to their following, the leaders have reduced themselves into shrill champions of castes, sub-castes and sub-sub-castes, religious groups and narrow political factions. Each of the self-declared spokesmen of the group and sub-group is more anxious than his internal rivals to retain his following within the relevant group.

These self-appointed *lilliputs* are mere reflectors of the immediate and narrow self interests as well as the anxieties and prejudices of their following. They are very much like the litmus paper turning red or blue in response to the surrounding milieu. After winning *Home Rule*, over the decades the political contest as to *who will rule at home* grew narrower at the base, nastier all over the country and of late violent and literally deadly. Some of this was inevitable. But the degree and the extent of degeneration are simply mind-boggling. The local elections in Andhra Pradesh held in June-July 2006 are only the most recent episodes of national shame. Each election seems like that we have hit the lowest possible levels in public morality. But, the next one gets worse! While elections in the Nehru Era were not free from blemishes, what we see today is simply despicable. The concepts of legacy and heritage, in the contemporary context, must be admired as the beautiful flowers that rise above the underlying mud and mush in the lake.

Foreign Policy

Change is the law of life and legacies are not for ever. Each generation has to modify (add, subtract and enhance) them into a living heritage to meet the challenges confronting the nation from time to time. This is not an easy task and demands a proper appreciation of the eternal and the ephemeral, the enduring and the transient in the inherited legacy. Neither protecting nor preserving *the essence* demands the courage of conviction, not the calculation of costs, or winning at any cost. Discarding the non-essential or the incidental requires discrimination, the sagacity to choose, sift the grain from the chaff. It is from this perspective, I want to examine closely the Nehruvian legacy of our foreign policy – its rationale, underlying philosophy, overarching purpose and what (if any thing) remains as our heritage today.

Let me at the outset assert in no uncertain terms that Nehru's foreign policy was the national foreign policy and remained so for long years. No democratic leader in history probably enjoyed wider popular support than Nehru as the architect of his country's foreign policy. It is no exaggeration to say that everybody, his grandmother, and her kissing cousins in the vast land of ours endorsed it, nay acclaimed it at every turn. Barring a few consistent dissenting voices (Rajaji, Minoo Masani) and a few other 'nay sayers', the whole nation applauded Nehru's foreign policy consistently, year after year, and for long years. Let me also add the almost all the scholars, sundry analysts and media pundits all over the nation were very much an integral part of the overwhelming democratic mandate Nehru enjoyed over his foreign policy and much beyond, till the border debacle of 1962.

It is worth recalling that Nehru pointed out that the foreign policy he advocated was ordained by the historical context of the times, India's cultural heritage and civilization. Anyone else in his situation would have followed the same policy, he declared time and again. We as a free nation came into a world we had not done much to create. Long before we became independent, we were anti-colonial, anti-imperialist and anti-racist. The three powerful emotive negatives defined our very consciousness, which naturally governed and shaped our foreign policy in the formative years. That was also the early phase of the cold war between the two super powers of the day. Since we became free from the colonial West, there was no question of our joining that camp.

The Communist Party of the Soviet Union *officially* characterised Gandhi and Nehru as *the running dogs imperialism.* Naturally, we were averse to be with Stalin's Russia. Since we became newly independent, we were particularly anxious to guard our newly won freedom. We were very touchy about any hint of our being less than free on any score or at any time. We had no choice but to hew an independent path as best as we could and protect it from the distracting forces and factors at work. Furthermore, the proverbial *middle path* was in tune with our philosophy of moderation and suited our temperament of avoiding extremes (*ati sarvatra varjayet*). Thus, to pursue an independent course of action in external relations is *the eternal* element in the Nehruvian legacy of our foreign policy. The historical compulsions to hew an independent path and the passion to be free, to be autonomous (and not to be a mere camp follower) subsequently evolved into the foreign policy of non-alignment, as will be explained shortly. Nonalignment was the conceptual response and the Non-Aligned Movement (NAM) was the institutional strategy to build a niche for our autonomous foreign policy and to win the support of the Third World countries.

At this stage it is vital to bring in the unique additional dimensions of the Nehruvian legacy in the years immediately following our emergence as an independent nation. In addition to the assertion that we would pursue a truly free and independent foreign policy, under Nehru's leadership we declared that India would make common cause with all the subjugated and exploited people everywhere. We promised them (and ourselves) that we would fight for their freedom, upliftment and well-being. Many a leader and vast segments of people in Asia and Africa those days looked up to Nehru and India because we went through the same ordeals, our heart and soul were with them, and we championed their cause wholeheartedly (and at times at the expense of our own nation state interests). India stood for something noble and unique. India promised them (and ourselves) that we would speak up for the South in the North-South equation and we could be trusted. These and other such nuances of policy and values we stood for were as much an essential ingredients of the Nehruvian legacy in foreign policy as the foundational principles of autonomy, freedom and sovereign independence.

But, somewhere along the line we lost our way. We drifted away from our idealism. Concern for other nations and peoples was downgraded. Consequently, we lost our representational legitimacy as the spokesman of the poor people and the poor countries in the world. We degenerated into a run of the mill "nation state" in tune with *the realist* mystique of the West. We got sucked into the extant balancing game of the super powers. We *matured* into a pragmatic nation state protecting our *national interests* (territory, power, security, ego, economic interests of the ruling elite, etc.). But, in the process we became acculturated and began to play the game of international politics as best as any of the regulars on the beat! All this was explained away and stoutly defended as realism, as growing up in the real world of sovereign states (*scorpions in the bottle* syndrome).

It is usually forgotten that *realism* is only a theory of reality and it is as valid as any of the many other theories seeking to explain the complex reality on the ground, the *real* world, and the nature of man. To insist that man is in reality a beast, selfish, power hungry and nothing else is indeed inadequate, wrong, and not justified. Only the not so good samples of mankind propagate such a devilish theory of man's nature. Man is also good, helpful, God fearing, and is also ready to sacrifice (even his life) for the sake of his dear ones, his country and fellow men. What is needed is the right leader in right place at the right time, as was demonstrated by the Mahatma. In the jargon of political science, however, Mahatma Gandhi was an extra constitutional source of power and influence in Indian government and politics. So was Sanjay Gandhi! It is needless to add that there is nothing common between them, except the happen stance of the common surname. The Mahatma was an incarnate of idealism, sacrifice and justice. The other Gandhi was not holding these values.

It is necessary to recall a bit of history here, however quickly. The early phase of the Nehru legacy in our foreign policy, i.e., the passionate espousal of freedom and vociferous upholding of the country's sovereign independence ended abruptly in 1954. I am sure all of us know the profound significance of the chronological divide, i.e., Pakistan's entry into the SEATO, and the global American Military Alliance system, and the consequent induction of the cold war into our immediate neighbourhood. By then the Soviets cobbled up a military alliance system of their own to counter the US and the West. It is then that India began enunciating the policy of non-alignment vis-à-vis the two military blocs led by the super powers. That is how we got sucked into the paradigm of the no holds barred global confrontation (short of war) between the Big Two. No doubt we were sincerely against the whole cold war syndrome and said so openly, loudly and with moral indignation every now and then. But, we were compelled to define our policies and actions in relation to the extant cold war context. We did not have much choice. The policy of non-alignment was conceptually and locationally situated in relation to the overarching framework of the East-West conflict raging all over the world. Non-alignment quickly turned into a complex and elaborates exercise in maintaining equal distance from the two power blocs. This circus of maintaining equi-distance between the Big Two went on for some years.

Nehru and the lesser leaders in the public arena felt compelled to balance every condemnation of the one side by a similar damnation of the other, that too at the earliest immediate opportunity that came along. This posture of plague on both sides soon became a national past time. This exercise in balancing gradually became a so mechanical and cleverer by half that when we failed to condemn both sides equally vehemently for similar wrong doings, we declared that *we judge all issues on their merits!* I am sure the older members in the audience can easily recall the phrase and refrain of those times. There is also no need for me to dilate on the elaborate intellectual exertions the academic explicators of India's foreign policy went through in the halcyon years of non-alignment to *justify* everything we said and did on the foreign policy front. As always, ingenuity in hair splitting was certainly not in short supply in the academic world of India.

We condemned capitalist and socialist military interventions and armed actions in foreign lands vehemently, almost equally so! However, our heart was on the left side and we gave the Soviet Union the benefit of doubt (a bit too often). I can easily recall the intellectual gyrations and the cerebral gymnastics performed by the archpriests of non-alignment those days stoutly defending all actions and each every pronouncement of Nehru and the Government of India. Every shift and turn, nuance and re-formulation, action and retraction was explained away and cleverly fitted into the ever commodious quilt called non-alignment. Finally, the conceptual quandary was resolved cleverly by asserting that non-alignment was whatever Nehru and India said, or did! The absurdity of such a formulation did not deter the faithful. I am sure our friends assembled in the hall and many of their senior colleagues not present here recognise the pervasive reality of those days.

Explaining the philosophy of nonalignment, defending it passionately, and dilating on the why and how of the Non-Aligned Movement, and the great and pivotal role India played on the world scene as the mediator between the Big Two grew into a huge academic enterprise in India, with its headquarters in Delhi and manned by scores of illustrious *Sarkari Intellectuals* scattered through out this vast land of ours! Non-alignment assumed all the trappings of a faith, an established Church. Not praising non-alignment was not acceptable, a not done thing! (I know of a distinguished Ambassador, a career official who made it to the top, but failed to get the next posting because of the less than kind words he uttered about non-alignment (in private) trickled back to Delhi through the diplomatic grapevine). In fact everyone singing praises of non-alignment and extolling Nehru, its architect, was one of the negative aspects of the reporting from our embassies and chancelleries around the world those days.

After 1962 non-alignment blossomed into bi-alignment. Equi-distance was transformed into equal proximity vis-à-vis both the power blocs. When the Chinese soldiers came down the Himalayas and pushed our armed forces southward mile after mile, the US came to our rescue in a big way and very quickly. India welcomed and received the massive and timely military help from the Americans with unaccustomed warmth and unalloyed enthusiasm. Khrushchev looked the other way when the Chinese asked for help in the war against India. For the first time in the history of international communism, a communist state did not support a fraternal communist country in its war against a non-communist nation! Mao's China heaped choicest abuses on Khrushchev. He was called *the revisionist* and a *paper tiger* (the worst term of abuse in the communist lingo those days), because Khrushchev suddenly bolted from the Cuban missile crisis raging at the same time on the other side of the globe. Kennedy and Khrushchev retreated from the brink of a nuclear disaster and chose to return to sanity. A *Hot Line* was quickly put in linking Washington and Moscow so that the Big Two could talk things over to avert similar crises in future. Chinese saw the writing on the wall and quickly announced a unilateral ceasefire. They cleverly declared that their military mission against India accomplished its goals!

The next big event in the emergence of India as an area of agreement between the Big Two was the Tashkent Agreement of 1965. India and Pakistan went to war against one another one more time. This time it was the turn of the Soviet Union to play the midwife in delivering a cessation of hostilities and a peace accord. The Americans seemed to say to the Soviets, we have had enough! You are most welcome to the headaches of keeping India and Pakistan from each other's throat. Russians succeeded in ironing out an agreement between the two countries and the rest is history, as they say.

In the bargain non-alignment became more helplessly integrated into the paradigm of the super power politics. By now our original commitment, the Nehruvian legacy of pursuing a free and independent foreign policy passed through several forms. Its chronological allotropy may be dubbed as non-alignment, equidistance, equal proximity and bi-alignment. The next and probably the final phase came with the collapse of the Soviet Union and the end of the cold war. One pole in the bipolar world collapsed and went out of the reckoning. Non-alignment became irrelevant and conceptually meaningless. There is only one super power on the global scene and all nations had to evolve their own equation with the mightiest nation in human history in their own way. The cold war and non-alignment passed into history. But that does not necessarily mean that people and governments accept the logic of reality openly or in good faith. No wonder the perorations regarding non-alignment being alive and re-re-assertions of its robust health continue. It is still the ruling doctrine of our foreign policy. But, eventually, reality will catch up with even the blindest espousers of non-alignment!

Let us recall that when we began as a nation our overarching original goal was to make our teeming millions (now a billion and growing) less hungry, less naked, and less poor. Then we were radical and passionately committed to our own freedom and that of all the people all over the world. We were also honestly committed to the destruction and elimination of the dependency structures everywhere, whether they were under western capitalism or neo-colonialisms of the new vintage. Then our bark was stronger than our bite. Our passionate advocacy of the New International Economic Order (NIEO) and the New International Information Order (NIIO) during the 1960s and 1970s are mere memories of a bygone era.

Now we are *less naked, less hungry, and less poor* than ever before. In fact India is now billed as the third biggest economy and is growing bigger each passing month. We are no more a mere regional subedar. India is now global player in its own right and is admittedly so by all accounts. Our bite therefore can be bigger and have more teeth. But, alas, the will to bite is gone. The passion to fight for the poor at home and in other countries has disappeared. The early idealism is missing and the spark is gone. We are too busy feathering our own nest, as a nation, as leaders and as individuals. Greed is order of the day. Grab what all you can and a bit more whether you need it or not, is the norm.

In public and in our class rooms we talk endlessly of interdependence of the world, about the juggernaut of economic integration and globalisation. There is even glib talk of the conceptual and operational obsolescence of the sovereign nation state in the globalizing world of ours today. Yet, when it comes to our own country and our foreign policy, we hark back to the 18th and 19th centuries. If we are living in a global village, should we not have the intellectual integrity and the fortitude to act on that premise? Purely nationalistic and narrowly self-centred approaches are obsolete, illogical in the 21st century, we all preach in theory. From the perspective of the welfare of mankind as a whole, sustainable development for all, and the ecological future of the planet, narrow nationalism of the 19th century vintage is not merely obsolescent, but positively dysfunctional. There is every danger of mankind *progressing* towards the exhaustion of the planet into oblivion!

If we as a nation insist that the North should share its wealth with the South, is it alright for us to drive the hardest bargain with Bangladesh, Nepal or Maldives? Should not the rich Indians share their wealth with their fellow citizens, who are poor and have to eke out a living? The Africa Fund came 50 years too late. Not long ago we used to inveigh against the Military Industrial Complex in the US and denounce the arms exporting nations as *Merchants of Death*. India under the spell of the latest mantras of liberalisation, privatisation and globalisation, is anxious to join the elite arms exporting club. We want to make our not so pretty a penny selling sophisticated weapons to poor countries and not so democratic regimes all over the world. We also want to buy weapons of mass destruction from the established merchants of death, who are a lot bigger and more *advanced* than us in the commerce of death. India is among the top five/six nations in terms of the weapons market (selling and buying). Big deals have big scope for lots of loose cash. There is no need to jolt our memories with the jeeps and coffee makers of the Krishna Menon fame, Jaugars of Jayjivan Ram vintage, and of course the guns of Bofors, that refuse to fall silent even off the battlefield!

Can we discard the ephemeral in the Nehru Legacy and revitalise the eternal in it? Can we regain the passion and the commitment of the early years of our Independence and internationalise our foreign policy? Though we are an independent sovereign nation with rich heritage going back to centuries, we as a country are getting lost in the enveloping sea of aping the West. We know that liberal capitalism, especially the brand championed by the US, is ugly and unjust. We know that profit driven growth is simply not concerned with equity. We know that such growth will not eliminate poverty, nor ameliorate the socio-economic inequities in the society. Otherwise, poverty should have disappeared from USA long ago. In fact the problem of poverty in America today is as intractable as ever. The rich-poor divide within and between countries has widened in the wake of the capitalist globalization sweeping the globe. To hold the contemporary western society as the best possible model humans can devise, I sincerely believe, is and should be a testament to the bankruptcy of man's ingenuity and his much flaunted knowledge society of the 21st century!

Let me conclude by saying that like all legacies, the Nehruvian legacy did not escape the ravages of time and change. But, there are many eternal strands in it that are worthy of preservation and revitalization. His idealism and concern for the welfare of all, selflessness, and faith in scientific spirit and modernity should become the guiding principles for this ancient land once again. But, looking at the state of affairs in the country, no one can be optimistic about the revival of the eternal in the Nehruvian legacy in the country.

10

Jawaharlal Nehru's Dialectics

R.L.M. Patil

As a speaker and writer Pt. Jawaharlal Nehru was a gifted person. He had his own way of convincing his readers and listeners of the correctness of his opinion. He did this through a method of arguing against himself. He invited his audience to share his inner dialogue. He did not appear to attack his detractors headlong. Instead he appears to agree with his opponent's viewpoint in the beginning of his argument. In the end, however, he shows his opposition and takes a stand which was more of a reconciliatory nature than scoring a triumphant point. He appears to absorb contradictions rather than breakdown the conflict. His well stated positions on several important issues can be cited to prove this skill of his. Some of these are: India's position on the Kashmir question, India-China border problem, Commonwealth, States reorganization, Socialism for India, Judiciary Vs. Parliament, Relevance of Gandhi, and his own role as Prime Minister vis-à-vis his cabinet ministers. One finds that in all these Nehru is not *prima facie* consistent in his views or even self-contradictory.

A deeper examination would, however reveal that he was in argument with himself, unable to take a fundamental/ultimate position. He was preparing his defence in advance in case of failure of his approach. He was both this and that: a queer mixture of both the stated positions. To take but two examples—one small another big—one may examine Nehru's position on India's membership of the Commonwealth of Nations, and socialism which was the corner stone of his ideology throughout his political career. Prior to Independence Nehru was unusually harsh on the imperialist import of the British Commonwealth of Nations. As quoted by S. Gopal in his first volume of Nehru's biography pp. 352-353, Nehru said in December 1946: "Under no conceivable circumstances is India going to remain in the British Commonwealth whatever the consequences. This is not a question for me to decide or for any few of us to decide. Any attempt to remain in Commonwealth will sweep away those who propose it and might bring about major trouble in India. We must, therefore, proceed on the assumption which is a practical certainty that India will go out of the British Commonwealth by the middle of next year." However the opposite happens.

At the concluding session of the Commonwealth in London on April 27 1949, India's Prime Minister endorsed the continued membership of India in the Commonwealth and asked the Constituent Assembly within a month [1] to ratify his stand. He treated it as a treaty commitment. Why this remarkable change in his attitude? Nehru would wax eloquent on the dropping of the prefix 'British' in the nomenclature of the Commonwealth of Nations to make his decision palatable to the Indian parliamentarians. But the British Prime Minister Mr. Attlee had stated in his reply to a query in the House of Commons only a few days earlier [2] that there was no official dropping of the 'British' in the Commonwealth association! Also, Nehru in his defence gave a long justification which was one-sided rather than a balanced judgment. It did not refer to his own unqualified opposition to the idea a few months earlier. However, he remembered the critics who openly questioned his sudden turn-around towards the end of his speech to the Constituent Assembly [3]: "(They) have been unable to come out of that cage of the past in which we all of us have lived, even though the door was open for them to come mentally out. They have reminded us, and some of our friends have been good enough to quote my speeches, which I delivered fifteen and twenty years ago. Well, if they attach so much value to my speeches, they might listen to my present speech a little more carefully.

The world has changed, Evil remain evil, and good is good; I do not mean to say that it is not; and I think imperialism is an evil thing and wherever it remains it has to be rooted out; and racialism is an evil and has to be fought. All that is true. Nevertheless, the world has changed; England has changed; Europe has changed; India has changed; everything has changed and is changing." And then he went on to make a small summary of three hundred years of achievements of Europe! Returning to his critics' harsh words against him he put up a brave moral posture: "I have certainly the capacity to use language, clever language to hurt people, and dialectical language, but I do not wish to use it..."

It was a clever tactic on his part to forgive his critics. But in the process of debate he forgot his own words uttered earlier. Had he changed his thinking for any good reason? He would not give a specific or honest reply. Instead he chose to go in a round about manner and referred to changes which have come about everywhere in Europe and the world (over the past three hundred years past!) and held out the philosophy of "being good to others will bring out good in them"

In the Parliament/Constituent Assembly Nehru had got a preponderant majority of members on his ruling party's side. He had no fear of losing any vote on the floor. Yet, he appeared to be labouring hard to prove his innocence, wisdom and the correctness of his reading the situation. In his defensive speech he was seen educating the minds of his Parliamentary colleagues more than meeting their objections. He carried the day with aplomb, without a doubt.

If one were to count his speeches on why there should not be linguistic reorganization of States, and then his justifications for reorganizing the States on the primary basis of language only, or his positions on Shiekh Abdulla or the plebiscite in J&K there would be no doubt in anybody's mind that he was adept in shifting his positions without being seen as contradictory personality. For every stance or stand he would produce a convincing argument. The positions would not be static or stagnant but flexible and dynamic. This mastery of movement of posture was peculiarly charming in the case of Nehru. This may be described in greater detail with respect to his 'socialist' philosophy.

The younger Nehru in London searching for an intellectual identity was enthused about socialism. In the 1920s and 1930s he was a self–styled socialist and a reluctant Gandhian. In his view, then, nationalism or national movement in India had to be married to socialism. His espousal of socialist cause made him the centre of attraction for all the young 'leftist' congressmen. His understanding of socialism at that time was brilliant yet bookish. It was romantic and appealing. It looked like typical Leninist, too, as it emphasized on nationalization of means of production and distribution by the state. Its ideology was the sole choice of the future in Europe as elsewhere. It was the cry of the poor, oppressed and the exploited. Nehru made it a point to prepare the Congressmen and the public in general to be ready to receive a massive dose of socialism when independence dawned. Yet he omitted to mention the name of socialism or any specific economic ideology of his preference in his address to the nation on the eve of independence. [4] Nor was socialism mentioned in the Preamble to the Constitution!

When he took over the reins of government he preferred to talk on the importance of economic growth and production rather than nationalization of property be it industry or agriculture. Often his socialist colleagues in the Congress were perplexed and peeved over his ambivalence and hesitation in declaring socialism as the official policy of the government. When they all walked out of the Congress, the party at his behest adopted (at its annual session at Avadi in January 1955) the famous resolution making the establishment of *socialistic pattern of society* as its goal. It won for Nehru a handsome electoral dividend but left the leftist in the country baffled. While the real socialists were in opposition, those who were bemused by the word socialism were in the treasury benches in the parliament.

Prime Minister Nehru was seen struggling to find balance between the attraction of ideology and compulsion of power. He was busy extricating himself from the dogmatic dimensions of socialism. He repeatedly came out with his new and often revised colourful ideological packages like 'equal opportunity' theory for "every man, woman and child," "egalitarian society" "removal of unemployment," "democratic socialism" "some middle way" "third way" "welfare state," "social change", "broad approach ", "Basic Approach", etc. But on the ground there was no visible change in the direction of socialism. As Ashok Mehta would say: To Jawaharlal, socialism was not a doctrine to be pursued but only a slogan to become popular. Or, as Prof. Hiren Mukerjee put it: "The Bhuvaneswar session [5] witnessed a generous proliferation of socialist semantics but neither its resolutions nor its other documents or speeches presented an intellectual doctrine or a programme of action." This, nine years after the Avadi session! Nehru humbly accepted a while earlier in the Lok Sabha [6]: "If any Hon, Member on the opposite side criticized us for not having gone fast enough on the road to socialism I would accept that criticism, we have been slow for a variety of reasons." It was at this session that Nehru suffered a paralytic stroke from which he could not recover. If Chinese aggression on our border in October 1962 was one grave setback to his policy, this non-accomplishment on the socialism front was no less agonizing.

Yet in spite of his failure which was apparent, Nehru held on to his belief was socialism was the only choice before India, and indeed the whole world. Six months before his demise he would still urge the Lok Sabha [7]: "A socialist approach is inevitable. There is no other way. I submit to this House with great confidence that if we adopted the capitalist approach, it would lead us nowhere". Four months earlier [8] he had already told the House: "I am convinced that there is no choice for India, No party, whatever it may feel, can stop this country's march to socialism." This assertion has to be remembered with his own insistence way back in April 1956: "We want a socialistic pattern of society. That is a phrase which means, in one word, socialism. Do not imagine that it means anything other than socialism. A socialistic pattern is socialism."

He might as well have said: Socialistic pattern of society is *not* socialism as such! For, he was torn between the concept and reality of socialism. As one of the most a competent and sympathetic biographer of his from Russia Dr. Orest Martyshin says: "The Nehru of the late 1920s and early 1930s was a refutation of the Nehru of the 1940s-1960s". [9] Prof. R. Ulyanovsky in his introduction to this important work says without hesitation: "When Nehru became Prime Minister, the term 'Socialism' disappeared from his political parlance. And when later, in the mid-50s, the socialist slogan re-emerged on the political scene it was viewed quite differently, not in the revolutionary or national-democratic terms but in the spirit of reformism." He also understood how "one could easily blame Nehru for his inconsistency, for reneging on what he had himself advocated. On the whole he deserves this criticism, but...." [10]

Like these two admirers from socialist country, others too found Nehru a bit of puzzle. They thought he represented a greater puzzle that was India. The Editorial of the *Times of India*, which read like a profound treatise, published in its issue of November 14 1988 that is on his birth-centenary, acknowledged the difficulty of understanding Nehru properly. "Whenever he was faced with a choice between romantic revolutionism and hard-headed realism, he invariably chose the latter. Thus despite all his differences with Gandhiji beginning with Mahatma's decision to call off the disobedience movement on account of the Chauri-Chaura incident in the early twenties, Nehru preferred to abide by the Mahatma's leadership; he empathized with the congress socialists and even the communists often highly critical of Gandhiji, but he never joined them...." It further took the rhetorical line that "Nehru was exposed to contrary pulls and pressures for India itself are a vast contradiction. Nehru was not an integrated personality because India is not an integrated society."

Perhaps, Nehru would not disagree with this observation. For, he had expressed himself clearly on the same lines in his *Diary*, while he was in Ahmednagar Fort prison. On hearing that Gandhiji was planning to call off the Quit India agitation and going to meet the Viceroy, Nehru gave a free vent to his suppressed feelings. He wrote in his *Diary*:

"With all his very great qualities he has proved a poor and weak leader, uncertain and changing his mind frequently. How many times he has changed during these last four years since the war began? It is very sad, this deterioration of a very great man. The greatness remains in many ways, but the sagacity and intuitive doing of the right thing are no longer in evidence."

On August 5, 1944, still in prison Nehru wrote an even more caustic entry in his *Diary*:

"My mind goes back (to all those conflicts between me and Gandhiji from 1936-37 to the present). And now? All these explanations without end and toning down of everything—this groveling before the Viceroy and Jinnah- this maybe the satyagraha technique, if so, I fear I do not fit in at all- it does not even possess the saving grace of dignity- Tall talk and then excuses, explanations and humility".

"What I may do outside after our release, I do not know. But I feel that I must break with this woolly thinking and undignified action- which really means breaking with Gandhi. I have at present no desire even to go to him on release and discuss matter with him- what do such discussions lead to?"

And the beauty of his soliloquy is contained in his next short sentence: "I suppose I shall see him anyhow". [11] This entry, this feeling, this approach of Nehru vis-à-vis Gandhiji is an epitome of his dialectic method of interpersonal relationship. Genuine differences submerged in genuine affection. Thoughts were dissolved in feelings. The common concern for the society overarched the details of different assessments of events. As the *Times of India* editorial, mentioned above, concluded: "A civilization has to be internally consistent; it cannot be a patchwork. India remains a battleground of three civilizations. As an individual, Nehru too was such a battleground. He synthesized the competing civilizations better than most of us."

Perhaps the passing away of Gandhiji and Sardar Patel, and the distance which grew between Nehru and Jaiprakash Narain, Lohia, Kripalani, Rajaji and the other erstwhile colleagues of his in the freedom movement kept Nehru in isolation. The pigmies who surrounded Nehru might have contributed to the increased burden on his intellectual, physical and spiritual resources. He faltered under the unshared weight of the responsibility of guiding and administering the complex nation.

As Pascal once put it, "all our reasoning is in essence surrender to the feelings." In Nehru's case this remark seems to apply so aptly. It would not be far from truth to say that Nehru thought through his heart. His relative failure or success on any front has to be appreciated for the immense honesty of thoughts preceding it. How he expressed his feelings and thinking was a matter that could be debated. Was it straight, or was it convoluted, or was it artfully concealed? Perhaps he was negotiating with himself. It was a loud-thinking on his part through which he wanted to educate the public. It may even be said that it was his dialectic process of thought and movement.

Notes

1. Jawaharlal Nehru's speech on May 16, 1949.
2. Jawaharlal Nehru's speech on May 2, 1949.
3. Jawaharlal Nehru's speech on May 17, 1949.
4. Jawaharlal Nehru's speech on September 7, 1946.
5. Jawaharlal Nehru's speech on January, 1964.

6. Jawaharlal Nehru's speech on August 22, 1963.
7. Jawaharlal Nehru's speech on December, 1963.
8. Jawaharlal Nehru's speech on August 22, 1963.
9. Orest Martyshin (1989), Jawaharlal and his Political Views, Moscow, Progress Publishers, p. 222.
10. Ibid., p.11.
11. See, S. Gopal, Selected Works of Jawaharlal Nehru, Volume 13.

11

Nehru, Democracy and the North-East

Sudhir Jacob George

Jawaharlal Nehru was an outstanding politician, one of the greatest leaders of the national liberation movement, a champion of peace, democracy and social progress, a sworn enemy of social injustice and all types of oppression. Under Nehru's guidance, India was recognized into states according to national, ethnic and linguistic factors, thus ending the British administrative system, based on the principle of 'divide and rule'. The feudal division of the country was abolished and initial agrarian reforms were implemented, undermining the power of the big landowners. Nehru led the restructuring of the economy along the lines of a planned economy, and started the policy of industrialization which was decisive for the country's economic growth. Nehru's initiative led to the creation of a powerful and strengthening state sector. He was thorough-going democrat, fighter for equality, an opponent of caste, tribe and religious distinctions. Nehru was a staunch advocate of lasting national unity in India, based on a combination of the principles of democracy and centralism.

Nehru as India's first Prime Minister had to grapple with several intractable problems, this was more so in the frontier areas of the North-East wherein some of the tribal communities in particular the Nagas had outrightly rejected incorporation into the Indian Union, claiming that they were distinct people and were never directly a part of even the erstwhile British India. Although the Nagas under Z.A. Phizo declared independence in 1949 and later revolted and waged war against the Indian State, Nehru being a democrat and a strong supporter of the marginalized communities never advocated a military solution to the Naga problem.

In fact he opined, "The Nagas were a tough people who could give much trouble and Nehru saw the danger of any hurried attempt to absorb their areas into standard administration. Between this and the isolation of the British days there was a mid way, a friendly rather than coercive attitude, an acceptance of their social structure, protection from encroachments and advance in fields as education. He was of the firm resolve that they should neither be treated as anthropological specimens nor drowned in the sea of Indian humanity. They could not be isolated from the new political and economic forces sweeping across India, but it was equally undesirable to allow these forces to function freely and upset the traditional life and culture of the Nagas. It was presumptuous to approach them with an air of superiority and try to make of them second rate copies of people of/in other parts of India". In this regard, Nehru, while authorizing the Government of Assam to reject the demand for independence and to make clear that incitement to violence would not be tolerated, Nehru emphasized the importance of dealing with this problem in a psychological rather than political manner and instructed that punitive measures should be as far as possible avoided. [1].

During March 1952, Nehru met Z.A Phizo and told him bluntly that he would not listen to any talk of independence but was prepared to help the Nagas to maintain autonomy in cultural and other matters and he assured non-interference. [2] Nehru had no doubt that it was right in itself as well as politically expedient to create among the tribes a feeling of kinship with the rest of the country. "The movement for independence among the Nagas is entirely based on the assumption that Indians are foreigners ruling over the tribes. Our policy should aim at removing this impression. They should feel part of India and shares in its destiny but free to live their own lives, with opportunities to advance along their own line. [3]

Nehru insisted on a gradual spread of administration and its adoption to local conditions. Nehru would have slowed the pace of administrative penetration even more but for the necessity created by these tribal areas also being border areas. However he laid emphasis on the presence of Government being imposed more in the form of roads, dispensaries, schools, than in enforcing law and order. He directed that a cadre of senior officials, specially selected and trained for these areas, be built up and their subordinates be drawn from the local tribes. He stated "a feeling should be created among the Nagas that responsibility would be cast on them increasingly and that the authorities regarded them as partners in development". [4]

At the political level, the kind of solution he had in mind was not a Naga province within India but a district with greater autonomy so as to give a sensation of self government and check the widely resented growth of Assamese influence and control of the local economy. But neither prongs of Nehru's policy made any marked impression, because of the inertia of the Government of Assam and he had to concede later that the effort to win over the people of these areas had failed. [5] In fact the law and order approach had become the norm that persists even today and this could not/ cannot be the basis of any policy especially in a democracy. The result has been adverse though not surprising, the non-cooperative attitude of the Nagas. There was a greater demand for delinking of the Naga areas from Assam, this Nehru felt if not controlled/diluted might add to feeling against India. [6] Nehru felt one way of initiating a friendly and constructive approach was to extend the community project to tribal areas, to be followed by more positive action. Nehru stated "we are in a deadlock and we should explore ways of getting out of it". [7]

He believed, "vis-à-vis the Nagas the middle course between a complacent approach to the problem and an over dramatized approach, we must processed calmly sans excitement, sans shouting and yet with strength". [8]

With mounting rebellion and killing of army officers the officials in the Government of India, wanted a military solution. Nehru vetoed suggestions for machine gunning from the air. He opined suppression of revolt was the first step to be taken but obviously could not be the only one. Once the resistance was broken, political approach was to be renewed. Although time for this at that juncture was not ripe he held but he cautioned the army and civil authorities that nothing should be done which would widen the gulf between the Government and the Naga people. He said "we must not judge as we would others who are undoubtedly part of India. Nagas have no such background or sensations and we have to create that sensation among them by our goodwill and treatment. We shall have to think how we can produce this impression and what political steps may be needed. [9] He further opined it must always be remembered that if the Nagas are made to feel that they have no other alternative but to fight and die, they will prefer doing so. We must give them a better alternative and seek their cooperation or at least of those who are prepared to cooperate. This has not so far been done by the Assam Government or our military". [10]

Nehru was clear that there was no question of political or any other form of surrender to a small group in active revolt. Weakness in dealing with such revolt was a sin for Nehru. However he felt the military approach while needed was not adequate. Nehru insisted that soldiers and officials should always remember that Nagas were fellow countrymen who were not be merely suppressed but had to be won over. He felt that the Nagas should be permitted the fullest freedom subject to two overriding demands of national security and unity. How this is to be worked out remains a major problem even today in the North-East in particular, Nagaland, Manipur and Assam. (At that juncture postponement of a decision regarding Nagaland was a policy decision). Nehru had no intention of making a precise commitment until the revolt ended by the Nagas. The Naga problem remains intractable, especially with the demand of the Nationalist Socialist Council of Nagaland for Nagalim (Greater Nagaland) incorporating all the Naga inhabited areas in Manipur, Assam and also Myanmar. The Government has failed all these years to solve the problem and arrive at a democratically acceptable solution to all as regards Nagaland. It is hoped that the different stages of talks in Geneva between the representatives of NSCN and the Government of India will lead to the establishment of permanent stable peace and an acceptable democratic solution to the long drawn Naga imbroglio.

Besides his humane approach towards the Naga problem, the greatest contribution of Nehru to the North-East and its distinct people has been his formulation of five fundamental principles, popularly known as *Panchsheel* in relation to the North-East Frontier Agency (NEFA) He stated "people should be enabled to develop along the lines of their own genius and we should avoid imposing anything on them. There should be encouragement in every way for their own tradition, art and culture. Tribal rights in land and forests should be respected. Efforts should be made to build up a team of the indigenous people to do the work of administration and development. Some technical personnel from outside will no doubt be needed, especially in the beginning, but the introduction of too many outsiders into tribal territory must be eschewed. These areas should not be over-administered nor should they be overwhelmed with a multiplicity of schemes. We should work through and not in rivalry to their own social and cultural institutions. Results of growth and development should not be judged on the basis of statistics or the amount of money spent, but by the quality of human character that is evolved".

During the formative years of the Indian state towards formulation of policy in particular for the tribal areas of our North-East there was a clear divide between the assimilationists and the Nehruvian liberals. The assimilationists argued against Scheduled Areas and Autonomous Councils. They adverted to national unity stating "we should proceed in such a way that all different communities may vanish and we may have one nation, the Indian nation. [11] In response the Nehruvian liberals argued that national unity is reinforced through accommodation not imposition; that certain tribal cultures are more egalitarian than the dominant mainstream culture, and that arrogance and disrespect underline blanket statements regarding *our culture*. The Nehruvian liberals dominated the Constituent Assembly and won the debate and the Sixth Schedule providing for the establishment of Autonomous Councils, was adopted. Nehru's ideals for the North-Eastern region as manifest in his Panchsheel for NEFA are reflected in the Autonomous District Councils set up under the Sixth Schedule.

The Autonomous District Council (ADC) governed by the Sixth Schedule of the Constitution is a comprehensive indicator of the integrationist approach in India. The population of the areas that came under the ADC's was around 80 percent tribal. The ADC's are intended to be a mechanism whereby distinct tribal practices could be supported simultaneously such that those communities secured access to individual oriented political institutions. The sub-committee led by Gopinath Bordoloi of the Sardar Vallabhai Patel Advisory Committee on the Fundamental Rights of minorities, tribal areas *et al* of the Constituent Assembly that went into the specific requirements of the tribes of the North-East while opining that it is in everyone's interest to incorporate all Indians into a single representative system felt that a period of substantial autonomy at the District level in tribal areas would enhance that process, while at the same time offering a reasonable compromise for those people in the North-East, who sought complete independence from India as well as Britain. [12] The Bordoloi sub-committee report-incorporating Nehru's ideals for the North Eastern region included detailed provisions for ADC's in erstwhile excluded areas of Assam.

As compared to all other institutions of Indian national incorporation, ADC's were closest to the pure integrationist position. Council members to be freely elected but majority would be tribals and the Chief Executive Member was to be elected by the council members had mandatorily to be a tribal. However to offset the pre-dominance of tribals in the council, the Governor was to nominate two members and they were to be non-tribals. The policies and programmes of the ADC's was to be implemented by an Executive Committee that comprised of the CEM and two other members-appointed by the Governor on the recommendation of the CEM.

Powers and Functions of the ADC

Legislative Powers: The District Councils power to make laws on certain subjects enumerated in the sixth Schedule i.e. laws on the allotment, occupation or use of or setting apart of land, other than reserved forests for grazing, residential or other non-agricultural purposes, regulating Jhum and other forms of shifting cultivation, establishment of town and village councils and determination of its powers and functions, village police, public health, sanitation appointment/succession of Chiefs, Headmen, money lending, trading by persons other than Tribals, the inheritance of property, marriage, divorce, and social customs.

Executive Powers: The District Councils are authorized to establish, construct and manage primary and middle schools (During 1990's the Government of Meghalaya took over this function from the ADC's due to the mismanagement of Primary Education); dispensaries, markets, cattle pounds, forests, roads, waterways and determine the language to be used as medium of instruction in schools. The Council has also the power to assess and collect land revenue, tax, buildings, levy tolls and taxes on profession, trades and employment. It can levy goods tax and tax on maintenance of schools and dispensaries. The Council has also a right for a share in royalties received by the state government from licenses and leases granted for extracting minerals. This has become a contentious issue with the new liberalization policy

of the Government of India. Besides ADC's and indigenous
tribal organisations are demanding the right of contracting
directly with external agencies.

Forest and mineral royalties finance 40 percent of ADC
budget for example in Khasi Hills and this rises to 60 percent
if state and central block grants are excluded. This extensive
reliance on resource royalties places undue pressure on a state
like Meghalaya's environment. The increased demand for
government sanctioned timber felling boosts ADC royalties
but unscrupulous producers and government officials collude
to facilitate illegal felling of trees. Limestone/coal is the most
important minerals in Meghalaya. Often quarrying of both
leads to environmental degradation by which land is twice
ravaged. The states coal supply is to last another century but
costs already have begun to tell in the form of acidic water and
further 40 percent of those employed in these mines are school
dropouts. The states three ADC's have no role in regulating
coal mines but they receive royalties; thus they have to cope
with the social and environmental dilemmas thrown up by the
haphazard mining industry.

Notwithstanding these shortcomings in economic
development ADC's do play an important role in development
of the community and the economy of the state.

Judicial Powers: The District Council has the power to
constitute village courts for trial of suits in which both parties
are tribals. Besides-these functions to the state government
can entrust certain functions to the ADC's as and when
required.

Social Impact of ADC's

The main function of the ADC's has been integration of
tribal communities into the Indian political system sans unique
external pressures on well functioning social systems. The
substance of tribal culture was not to change due to the
establishment of ADC's but tribal processes were to become
more consistent with broader Indian political institutions.

The ADC's have a social impact through their legislative capacity. For example in Meghalaya ADC's have begun codifying customary laws but have also crafted laws that are rather in consistent with the customs. Though it has classified traditional tribal political processes but by doing so has transformed the very process.

The ADC's have a significant social impact in the administration of justice. The Sixth Schedule provides for ADC's to administer the judicial disputes ranging from the smallest village disputes to capital punishment. However, that latter has never been operationalized in the North-East.

Conclusion

The Nehruvian goal of functional autonomy to the tribes of the North-East has to an extent been secured by the application of the provisions of the Sixth Schedule in most of the tribal districts of the North-East, with the exception of Nagalard which has ignored the Sixth Schedule and Arunachal Pradesh, which has opted for the Panchayati Raj system. The success of provisions of the Sixth Schedule in the form of the operation of the ADC's have led to the formation of Autonomous Councils in the tribal dominant district of Tripura as a part of the Tripura Accord of 1976 and the Bodo Accord of the 1990's leading to the formation of initially the BAC and now the Bodo Tribal Council for the Plains Tribes of the Bodo dominant areas of Assam's Kokrajhar and Darrang districts.

Although functionally weak, ADC's do have had a positive and substantial impact on the deepening of the democratic process. In addition to its effect at the grass root village level through the village councils and town committees and through them its indirect shaping of change in tribal political processes- a new layer in India's federal democracy has opened up new avenues for aspiring political leaders in the North-East. As a political institution and as a formal link to state political institutions, the ADC eases pressures by ethnic communities to resort to violence in pursuance of political objectives. Thus, ADC's the third tier of India's federal system, enable political representation and debate to take place in a more comprehensive manner than would have been possible at the state level.

The Sixth Schedule and its provisions whose main architect was Nehru has strengthened the democratic ethos, to a large extent in the strife torn North Eastern region since the past few decades. It is important to note that only democratic practices and dialogue/settlement on the basis of equity and justice that can solve the outstanding problems in our country particularly in the North-East. In this regard as the talks are on to secure a solution to the Naga tangle at Geneva and efforts are being made to dialogue with the United Liberation, Front of Asom, it is imperative to advert to the Nehruvian approach while dealing with the demands of the tribal groups in ferment in the North East. Further some of the long standing demands of the communities and people of the region viz, demand for repealing of the Armed Forces Special Powers Act (demanded by the civil society and groups in Manipur); demand for relocation of army camps away from civilian areas in the region merit serious, positive consideration by the Government of India. A positive step taken to address these grievances can go a long way in bringing the people of these disturbed states of the North-East closer to mainstream India. How long will the armed forces of our country train its guns against its own people?

Building up of a strong, democratic India alone can bring about security, peace and prosperity to every section and community not only in the North-East but every remote and far flung region of our country.

Notes
1. Nehru, J. Letter to Governor of Assam, J. Daultaram, 2 February 1951.
2. Nehru, J, Letter to Chief Minister of Assam, B.R. Mehdi, 13 March 1952.
3. Nehru, J, Letter to Governor of Assam, J. Daultaram, 4 April

1952.
4. Nehru, J, Letter on North-East Frontier Agency, 24 April 1953.
5. Gopal, S, (1979) Jawaharlal Nehru – A Biography, Vol II, 1947-1956, Delhi, OUP, p. 210.
6. Nehru, J, Letter on North-East Frontier Agency, 24 April 1953.
7. Nehru, J, Letter to Chief Minister of Assam, B.R. Mehdi, 9 March 1955.
8. Nehru, J, Letter to Chief Minister of Assam, B.R. Mehdi, from Bandung 21 April 1955.
9. Gopal (1979), op cit., p. 211.
10. Nehru, J, Letter to K. N. Katju, Defence Minister, Govt. of India, July 28, 1956.
11. Parliament of India, Debates, Constituent Assembly, Delhi, p. 985.
12. Hansaria, B.L., Sixth Schedule of the Constitution of India: A Study, Guwahati, Asok Publishers, pp. 183-229.

References
Jawaharlal Nehru's views on Administration of Tribal Areas of North-East in Hassan Amir (1988), *The Tribal Administration in India,* Delhi, B.R. Publishers, pp. 55-56.
The proposal for the Sixth Schedule of the Constitution of India was presented on September 5, 1949 and it was ratified on September 7, 1949.

12

Contextualizing Nehruvian Development: Democratic Compulsion and Political Reality

V. Bijukumar

Any development model which bound to operate in a liberal democratic set up may enshrine equity and justice. In other words, a development model in a liberal democracy does not function in a vacuum; it must respond to the aspirations and material needs of the people. As a matter of fact Nehruvian development can be seen and interpreted in a historical context. It was a product of a long process of interactions, compromises and the accommodation of diverse ideas and ideologies. Both 'time' and 'space' influenced Nehru in moulding his development model. The Nehruvian development is a product of both global economic thinking and domestic politics. Globally, the ideological conflict between communism and capitalism as represented by two power blocs influenced the Nehruvian development thinking. Domestically, Nehru as the leader of the Indian National Congress, which was a movement for national freedom, had to protect the interests of various social groups. In every policy issue, Nehru tried to maintain a balance between domestic and global compulsion by evolving a consensus within the nation.

Nehruvian development evolved during the nationalist movement. It is to be remembered that during the nationalist movement, the Congress emerged as the vanguard of the freedom struggle by adopting an 'inclusive' agenda; fighting against the colonial exploitation and finding solutions for the vulnerability of masses and protecting the interests of cross sections of the people. According to Shepperdson and Simmons (1988), as far as the realm of economic policy is concerned, the Congress has tended to favour two general approaches. Firstly, 'the espousal of a set of purposely vaguely defined, relatively uncontentious and on the whole rather anodyne objectives' [1] such as the commitment to emerge from underdevelopment, providing minimum material needs to the majority population and encouraging self-reliance all of which are consistent with the formal continuance of a pluralist society. Secondly, 'it has been to lay down an explicit programme of goals, but at the same time to build a series of officially or unofficially sanctioned 'safeguards' so as to minimize damage to the most highly prized interests and most powerful political constituencies'. [2]

During the nationalist movement, the basic idea behind the Nehruvian development thinking was the attainment of a developmental/interventionist state to modernize the backward society and the welfare of its social classes. For this, even India's dominant elites and policy makers favoured the creation of a self-reliant economy and a powerful state. [3] The bourgeois class extended its support to the Congress for achieving an interventionist state, which, it felt, was essential for the development of the indigenous bourgeois class. [4] However, Nehru, on his part, projected the attainment of an interventionist state before the masses as an instrument for development and modernization. In fact, the state visualized by Nehru had the potential to function with relative autonomy vis-à-vis the interests of the dominant class and the industrial and business groups.

The Indian National Congress as a movement for freedom played an important role in moulding Nehru's development thought towards justice and equity. The multi-class, caste, regional and religious nature of the nationalist movement under Gandhi forced the Congress to arrive at a social consensus on its economic policies and programmes. The idea was to provide social, economic and political justice and to ensure the dignity of the individual. In the 1930s, the major conflict on the development policy was not between the socialist and the capitalist but from within the Congress between the Gandhians and the Socialists. A milestone in the Congress' policies and strategies in the pre-independence era was the Karachi Resolution (1931) which can be viewed as a blueprint to independent India's development strategy. The Resolution called for an interventionist state that could ensure the economic rights of the people which thus gave the economic policies of the Congress a left-of-centre approach. [5]

With the adoption of Karachi Resolution, the socialists especially, Nehru, gained an upper hand in the economic policy of the Congress. However, the later years witnessed the accommodation of Gandhian ethos in the development strategy. The All India Congress Committee (AICC) meeting held in Varanasi in 1934 had affirmed that the Congress should also encourage village cottage industries even while going for state directed industrialization. Consequently, *swadeshi* or self-reliance became a major theme of the Indian National Congress during the nationalist movement. The leadership of the Congress realized the need for a modern industrial economy for the achievement of economic freedom and to fulfil the aspirations of the nation. Towards this direction, there were discussions in the AICC to set up a Planning Committee aimed at giving a substantial role to the state in the development of Indian industry.

Based on the Congress Working Committee (CWC) resolution of 1937, the National Planning Committee was set up in 1938 under the chairmanship of Jawaharlal Nehru. The industrial class, on its part, prepared the Tata-Birla Plan, popularly known as the Bombay Plan. The Plan called for the establishment of centralized planning, the imposition of rigorous economic controls, the development of heavy industry, and the introduction of radical agricultural reforms. Thus, in general, planning was envisaged as an instrument to achieve or to ensure the material well being of the people. Again, it was considered not only as an indication of a change in the Congress' ideological preferences; it was a prelude to the multi-class character of the party. [6] In fact, 'planning was not only a part of the anticipation of power by the state leadership of the Congress, it was also an anticipation of the concrete forms in which that power would be exercised within a national state'. [7] The leadership believed that the only solution for problems of the world as well as that of India lay in socialism. They saw independence as a precondition for the reconstruction of both the economy and polity. So, the development policy and the strategy of the Congress during this period were aimed at achieving growth with justice. Further, the leadership felt that since good economy was a precondition for good democratic politics, the economic well being of the social groups would consolidate the role of the Congress in Indian politics.

After independence, Nehruvian development thinking assumed centre stage in Indian public policy. The Nehruvian era can be considered be considered as the foundational stage of institution building in independent India. The all round presence of the developmental state and the experiment of democracy gave greater impetus to the development of political institutions. These political institutions under the patronage of the developmental state provided a framework to accommodate the demands of new classes in a democratic way. The Congress transformed itself into a political party and emerged as a major political institution in India. The policies and strategies of the party were geared towards building a self-reliant modern economy in which political freedom could be made meaningful for the masses. The Congress party, which was the ruling party, in its economic policies, argued for an interventionist state which sought to take an active role in the development process. The intention for strengthening such a state by the party was due to both domestic and global factors. Domestically, the Congress wanted to project its image as the inheritor of the multi-class, multi-caste mass movement and it needed the continued support of all sections of society.

Globally, it needed the assistance of the Soviet Union for the reconstruction of independent India, though India adopted a non-aligned path in the bipolarized cold-war era.

The post-independent Nehruvian development strategy was influenced by the pressure emanating from the international system, domestic political coalition and the influence of ideology. The dominant thinking among the policy makers of the newly independent nation states was the vital role the developmental state could play in institution-building during the formative years of development. Mainly, two events had contributed to the strengthening of a strong developmental and interventionist state in their development strategy in the post second world war period. Firstly, the strong nationalistic and anti-colonial nature of the movement, the Great Depression of the 1930s, the rise of Keynesian economic thinking and the Second World War revived the questions of the state, government policies, state-market relations, growth-distributive justice, etc. Secondly, the success of state planning in achieving rapid industrialization in the Soviet Union greatly influenced policy makers in the 1950s. [8] Subsequently, in the 1940s and early 1950s, 'development economics' emerged as a sub discipline in analyzing the dominant role of the state in the economic development of the developing countries. The state assumed the role of a 'visible hand' in the nation-building process by acting as an agency for the welfare of the people.

Nehru was influenced by the success of the Soviet experiment of centralized planning and by the emergence of *developmentalism* as a new philosophy of development policy. However he argued that India must evolve a model of her own, which was based on democratic socialism and aimed at mixed economy and economic planning. Nehru, in fact, tried to place his development agenda in the Congress party forum. In January 1948, at the AICC's Economic Programme Committee which met under the chairmanship of Nehru and proposed radical measures 'to bring about equitable distribution of the existing income and wealth and prevent the growth of disparities with the process of industrialization'. [9] The Industrial Policy Resolution of 1948 was another significant development in this direction. It emphasized, among other things, a progressively active role for the state in the development of industries coupled with a valuable role for private enterprises, properly directed and regulated. [10]

The Delhi Congress Session of 1951 declared that the Congress stood for the progressive extension of public sector to various fields of economic activity. Further, the private sector was to function in close accord with the public sector for the fulfilment of common national objectives. On December 21, 1954, Nehru stated in the Lok Sabha that 'the objective of our economic policy should be a socialistic pattern of society'. [11] However, the official confirmation of the Congress party's stand was made at the Avadi session of the AICC in 1955. The Avadi session adopted a resolution stating that the establishment of a 'socialist pattern of society' was the party's objective. And the party reached a consensus regarding its policies and strategies based on this objective. The aim was to create a mixed economy, a mixed polity and a mixed society. [12] However, the post-independent economic policy developed from a complex interaction between economic and political factors, mirrored a corresponding set of economic and political objectives. [13] It may be recalled that even before independence, when Congress formalized its economic strategy for the post independent India, political considerations were also a determinant factor along with economic calculations. For instance, the political circumstances after independence forced Nehru to move towards left-oriented policies. Further, politically, the Congress party under Nehru had to counter the Swantantra party for its pro-liberal and market-oriented approach. [14]

The Nehruvian development thought based on equity and justice was, in fact, a synthesis of all the major ideological currents that were in existence within the Congress party.

They were the Gandhian philosophy of Sarvodaya that advocated a self-sufficient village economy based on small-scale industries; the socialist doctrine as advocated by the western educated Congressmen like Nehru himself who wanted heavy industrialization and the dominance of the public sector and the third approach advocated by Sardar Vallabhai Patel and Rajendra Prasad based on private capital and market economy. [15] Nehru synthesized these three major ideological currents of the 1950s–the unrestrained free-market capitalism, modified welfare capitalism and the more radical communist model [16]-into his vision of economic development and political democracy.

The underlying philosophy and ideology of Nehruvian development thought were to give more role to the state in economic development and a subservient role to the 'market'. Nehru believed that poverty and hunger in India can be removed by means of strengthening the role of the state. Towards this direction Nehru geared towards centralized planning, commanding heights of public sector in the mixed economy and provision for public subsidies to various groups. Parekh (1995) argues that 'by setting up an extensive public sector Nehru gave the state a powerful economic base and a powerful economic presence which ensured it autonomy and guarded it against blackmail and manipulation by organized interests'. [17]

Nehru conceptualized planning as the first step towards the goal of a socialist society. At the same time, he regarded the democratic values of the capitalist society as indispensable for the full growth of a just society. He, therefore, tried to reconcile the virtues of these two extremes and arrived at a vision of a new society based on democratic socialism. The Second Five Year Plan laid the foundation for economic development known for its Nehru-Mahalanobis strategy. It envisaged a significant role for the public sector and stressed the need for heavy industrialization. The domestic and small-scale industries were given protection from competition. The

Industrial Policy Resolution of 1956 was another significant development in demarcating the role of public and private sectors in Indian development. The basic objectives of the economic policy as explicated in the Industrial Policy Resolution of 1956 were 'the commanding heights of the public sector over the private sector, faster expansion of basic and key industries, prevention of concentration of economic powers in private hands, regional balance and promotion of small-scale industry'. [18] Nehru thought that industrialization can bring social justice by removing poverty in India. In his view, industrialization should address the poverty of the people. Industrial progress should be benefited by vast majority of the people and not a few industrialists and capitalists. He argued that:

Raising the standard of living of the masses must be the first priority in any scheme of industrial advancement and not a subsidiary benefit that may follow from industrial reconstruction. [19]

It can be seen that 'the process of accommodation began with the formulation of the Second Five Year Plan and became fully established with the proclamation of the Industrial Policy Resolution of 1956'. [20] Though, the Industrial Policy Resolution of 1956 set out some principles of Nehru's philosophy, it retained sufficient ambivalence to placate the uncommitted elements. [21]

Nehruvian development thought not only laid the foundation for economic modernization but also social and political modernization in India. The modernization process initiated by Nehru had some peculiar characteristics vis-à-vis those initiated in other newly independent countries of the decolonized era. It had a kind of relative autonomy both at the domestic level as well as global level. Domestically it succeeded in bargaining with the traditionally upper and dominant castes and classes in the process of modernization. It has been suggested that Nehru stood for the replacement of culturally rooted rationality by formal rationality; for the replacement of the individuals as part of communities by the notion of individuals a unencumbered selves; for the replacement of collective, communitarian, affective, spiritual orientation by individualistic, calculative, contractarian values and finally, for the replacement of an undifferentiated value system by separate spheres of morality, art and science. [22] In the economic realm central planning and public sector were the major instruments of modernization.

As it has been argued that Nehruvian development thought based on justice and equity is the product of the compulsions of liberal democracy in India. However, the development thought benefited the Congress party rather than the masses at large. The Congress could manage to develop a patronage politics which strengthened its base among various social groups in India. For instance, the Congress when it came into power developed an elaborate structure of patronage distribution in a multi-class coalition in independent India. [23] The elaborate network of patronage in the forms of subsidies, credits and public sector envisaged within the political economy under the purview of the developmental state enabled the party to co-opt and absorb diverse social groups. By influencing the distributive policies of the government, the party could meet the demands of its social constituencies and this contributed to broaden its mass base. The government's soft budget constraints and the provision of public subsidies, to various sectors and the generation of employment through an expansive state sector, expanded the party support in different spheres of the society. [24] For example, the provision of large input subsidies to the farm sector in the form of fertilizers, power, seeds, and irrigation and support prices for farm products helped the party to ensure the support of the agricultural communities.

Planned development was a crucial part of the legitimating ideology of the Congress in power; and 'planning' as a domain outside politics, became an essential instrument for patronage politics. [25] It helped to find areas for resource allocation and

overall development of certain regions. The instrument of
development planning and other development programmes, by
extending active agencies for development of the society,
provided new social and economic opportunities. The
introduction of poverty alleviation programmes, the adoption
of redistributive measures, the launching of employment
generation schemes, the high expenditure on the poor,
programmes intended to empower socially marginalized
sections, rural development schemes, high allocation in social
expenditure, distribution of essential commodities through fair
price shops to the poor, etc. had helped the local leadership of
the party to approach the common masses and to expand its
support base at the local level. [26]

The disbursement and distribution of resources to the
intended and unintended beneficiaries were done through
various levels of government structures like the state
governments and local institutions like Panchayati Raj, most of
which were dominated by the Congress party. [27] Moreover,
an elaborate network of patronage created by the party through
the programmes of development planning enabled it to bargain
with various social strata in rural and urban areas for political
support. [28] Thus, the programme of development and
planning can be seen as one of the three ways by which the
Congress established its dominance and the progressive
expansion of its social base. [29]

While acknowledging the public sector enterprises, it
strengthened the role of the private sector in the economy, it.
The wide-ranging public sector provided job opportunities and
recruitment to professionals and developed the patronage of
the bureaucracy committed to the party. [30] The provision of
affirmative action policies in the public sector stand a
testimony to the government's commitment to the deprived
sections of the society and established its linkage with these
groups. It is considered that 'the pressure to use public
revenues as patronage not only stems from the heterogeneous
nature of India's dominant classes but also originates in the

need to maintain electoral support in a democratic polity'. [31] It has been argued that this strategy of consolidation depended on a dispersal of power and patronage than it did on ideological appeal or organizational loyalties. [32] Moreover, the network of patronage and distribution of resources, made it difficult to other parties to compete with the Congress. Its implication for the party politics was that the policies of the Congress not only developed a character of *one party dominance* but also countered the opposition parties electorally despite India being a multi party system. [33]

To conclude, Nehruvian Development is the product of both domestic compulsions and political realities of the nationalist movement and the subsequent post independent era. Nehruvian development was, in fact, reflected the textbook definition of development, providing different things to different people. However, this can be seen in the context of how a development policy is coming under pressure from both global and domestic compulsions, especially in a liberal democracy based on competitive party politics. Whatever might be the economic rationality behind the Nehruvian development, it forced to operate under the compulsions of political rationality.

Notes

1. Shepperdson Mike and Colin Simmons, eds. (1988) *Introduction* in Mike Shepperdson and Colin Simmons, The Indian National Congress and the Political Economy of India, 1885-1985, Aldershot, Avebury, p. 21.
2. Ibid.
3. Rudolph Lloyed I. and Susane Hoeber Rudolph, (1987) In Pursuit of Lakshmi: The Political Economy of the Indian State, Chicago, University of Chicago Press, p. 214.
4. Bibin Chandra, *The Indian Capitalist Class and Imperialism before 1947* in Bipan Chandra ed., (1983), Imperialism and Nationalism in India, Delhi, Vikas Publications. Sarkar, Sumit, Modern India 1885-1947, Delhi, Macmillan. Desai, A.R, (1984) India's Path of Development: A Marxist Approach, Bombay, Popular Prakashan.

5. AICC, Resolution on Economic Planning and Programme 1924-54, AICC, New Delhi, 1954. The resolution proclaimed that ending exploitation of the masses, political freedom of the starving million. It made demand for control by the state of key industries and ownership of mineral resources and control over exchange and currency policy so as to help Indian industries and bring relief to the masses. pp. 3-6.

6. Chakrabarty Bidyut, *Jawaharlal Nehru and Planning, 1938-41: India at the Crossroads,* Modern Asian Studies, Vol. 26, No. 2, 1992, p. 280.

7. Chatterjee Partha, (1993), The Nation and its Fragments: Colonial and Post-colonial Histories, Delhi, Oxford University Press, p. 201.

8. Desai, op cit., pp. 51-52. Rosen George, (1996) Economic Development in Asia, Aldershot, Ashgate Publishing Limited, p. 257. Rangarajan, C. (2000), *State, Market and the Economy: Shifting Frontiers,* Economic and Political Weekly, Vol. XXXV, No. 16, 15 April, 2000 p. 1387.

9. AICC, Report of the Economic Programme Committee, AICC, New Delhi, 1948.

10. Government of India, (1948) Industrial Policy Resolution-1948, Ministry of Finance, New Delhi.

11. Lok Sabha Debates, Vol. VII, No. 26, 21 December, 1954, p. 1773.

12. Kothari Rajani, (1976) Democratic Polity and Social Change in India: Crisis and Opportunities, New Delhi, Allied Publishers, p. 52.

13. Chaudhuri Pramit, *The Origins of Modern India's Economic Development Strategy* in Shepperdson and Simmons, (1988) op cit., p. 272.

14. Kaviraj Sudipta, *Democracy and Development in India* in Amiya Kumar Bagchi ed., (1995) Democracy and Development, London, Macmillan, p. 103.

15. Kochanek Stanely, (1974) Business and Politics in India, Berkeley, University of California Press, pp. 77-78.

16. Kaviraj Sudipta, *Dilemmas of Democratic Development in India,* in Adrain Leftwich ed., (1996) Democracy and Development: Theory and Practice, Cambridge, Polity Press, p. 117.

17. Parekh Bhikhu, *Jawaharlal Nehru and the Crisis of Modernisation* in Upendra Baxi and Bhikhu Parekh eds., (1995)

Crisis and Change in Contemporary India, New Delhi, Sage Publications, p. 44.

18. Government of India (1956), Industrial Policy Resolution 1956, Ministry of Finance, New Delhi.

19. Inaugural Address at the Seventh annual session of the All India Manufactures Conference, New Delhi, 14 April, 1947. Quoted as Selected Works of Jawaharlal Nehru, Vol. 2, New Delhi, Oxford University Press, p. 585.

20. Hardgrave Robert L. and Stanley A. Kochanek, (1986) India: Government and Politics in a Developing Nation, New York, Harcount Brace Jovanovich Publishers, p. 311.

21. Rangnekar D. K., *Industrial Policy*, The Economic Times, Annual Number, 1975, p. 24.

22. Pantham Thomas, (1995), *Gandhi, Nehru and Modernity* in Baxi and Parekh, op cit. p. 98.

23. Bardhan Pranab, (1986) The Political Economy of Development in India, Delhi, Oxford University Press, p. 78.

24. Kochar R..C., (1997) Congress and Socialism: Economic Programmes and Policies, Delhi, Anamika Publishers & Distributors, p. 168.

25. Corbridge Stuart and John Harriss, (2000) Reinventing India: Liberalisation, Hindu Nationalism and Popular Democracy, Cambridge, Polity Press, p. 57.

26. Kohli Atul, (1987) The State and Poverty in India: The Politics of Reform, Cambridge, Cambridge University Press.

27. Vanaik Achin, (1990) The Painful Transition: Bourgeois Democracy in India, London, Verso, p. 77.

28. Mitra Subrata Kumar, *Democracy and Political Change in India*, The Journal of Commonwealth and Comparative Politics, Vol. 30, No. 1, March, 1992, p. 16.

29. According to Kothari, the Congress party established its dominance in the political system in the early decades of development by a process of progressive expansion of its social base in three ways. Firstly, soon after independence, it engaged in a process of 'displacement' of its own elite structure by taking the socially and economically entrenched groups into its organization. Secondly, it initiated a process of social cooption, supplementing the higher caste; new sections were recruited and penetrated into local regions and strongholds of traditional authority. Thirdly, through its extended programmes of

development and planning. Kothari Rajni, Politics and the People: In Search of a Humane India, Vol. I, New Delhi, Ajanta Publications, p. 7.

30. Vanaik, (1989), op cit., p. 77.
31. Kohli, Atul, *The Political Economy of Development Strategies: Comparative Perspective on the Role of the State*, Comparative Politics, Vol. 19, No. 2, January, 1987, p. 239.
32. Kothari, (1989) op cit., p. 51.
33. Manor, James, *Parties and the Party System* in Atul Kohli ed., (1988) India's Democracy: An Analysis of Changing State-Society Relations, Princeton, Princeton University Press, p.66.

Index

Index